The Wedding Collection

High Voice

Compiled and Edited by Richard Walters

On the cover: Georgia O'Keeffe, *Calla*, Oil on board, 1924.
Private collection, southern state, 1998.

ISBN-13: 978-1-4234-1264-9
ISBN-10: 1-4234-1264-8

HAL•LEONARD®
CORPORATION
7777 W. BLUEMOUND RD. P.O. BOX 13819 MILWAUKEE, WI 53213

Visit Hal Leonard Online at
www.halleonard.com

Contents

Title   **Composer**

Classical/Traditional

6	Alleluja	Wolfgang Amadeus Mozart
14	Ave Maria	J.S. Bach/Charles Gounod
18	Ave Maria	Franz Schubert
22	Bist du bei mir (You Are with Me)	Gottfried Heinrich Stölzel – (previously attributed to J.S. Bach)
26	Dank sei Dir, Herr (Thanks Be to God)	Siegfried Ochs – (previously attributed to Handel)
31	Entreat Me Not to Leave Thee	Charles Gounod
38	Jesu, Joy of Man's Desiring	J.S. Bach
45	Let the bright Seraphim (from *Samson*)	George Frideric Handel
43	Let the bright Seraphim—trumpet part	
57	The Lord's Prayer	Albert Hay Malotte
62	Mein gläubiges Herze (My Heart Ever Faithful)	J.S. Bach
52	Now Thank We All Our God	arranged by Richard Walters
76	Panis Angelicus	César Franck
70	Pur ti miro, pur ti godo (from *L'incoronazione di Poppea*)	Claudio Monteverdi (realization by Richard Walters)

Broadway

84	All Good Gifts (from *Godspell*)	Stephen Schwartz
90	All I Ask of You (from *The Phantom of the Opera*)	Andrew Lloyd Webber/Charles Hart/Richard Stilgoe
81	And This Is My Beloved (from *Kismet*)	Robert Wright/George Forrest
100	The Greatest of These (from *Philemon*)	Harvey Schmidt/Tom Jones
95	More I Cannot Wish You (from *Guys and Dolls*)	Frank Loesser
104	Some Enchanted Evening (from *South Pacific*)	Richard Rodgers/Oscar Hammerstein II
108	Someone Like You (from *Jekyll & Hyde*)	Frank Wildhorn/Leslie Bricusse
112	Sunrise, Sunset (from *Fiddler on the Roof*)	Jerry Bock/Sheldon Harnick
122	Till There Was You (from *The Music Man*)	Meredith Willson
117	Unexpected Song (from *Song & Dance*)	Andrew Lloyd Webber/Don Black

Standards

126	All the Way	James Van Heusen/Sammy Cahn
129	Fly Me to the Moon	Bart Howard
132	I Could Write a Book	Richard Rodgers/Lorenz Hart
135	Let It Be Me	Gilbert Becaud/Mann Curtis/Pierre DeLanoe
140	The Promise	David Shire/Alan and Marilyn Bergman
143	Starting Here, Starting Now	David Shire/Richard Maltby Jr.
146	Time After Time	Jule Styne/Sammy Cahn
149	Walk Hand in Hand	Johnny Cowell
152	The Way You Look Tonight	Jerome Kern/Dorothy Fields
155	With a Song in My Heart	Richard Rodgers/Lorenz Hart

Pop/Rock Classics

158	Annie's Song	John Denver
168	Endless Love	Lionel Richie
176	Grow Old with Me	John Lennon
165	Here, There and Everywhere	John Lennon/Paul McCartney
180	I Will	John Lennon/Paul McCartney
183	In My Life	John Lennon/Paul McCartney
189	We've Only Just Begun	Roger Nichols/Paul Williams
186	You Are So Beautiful	Billy Preston/Bruce Fisher
192	You Raise Me Up	Brendan Graham/Rolf Lovland

Contemporary Christian

204	How Beautiful	Twila Paris
212	I Will Be Here	Steven Curtis Chapman
197	If You Could See What I See	Geoff Moore/Steven Curtis Chapman
218	Love of My Life	Jim Brickman/Tom Douglas
236	My Place Is with You	Michael Puryear/Geoffrey Thurman
222	Parent's Prayer	Greg Davis
226	This Day	Jadon Lavik
232	This Is the Day	Scott Wesley Brown

INDEXED

Contents

Alphabetically by Title

84	All Good Gifts (from *Godspell*)	Stephen Schwartz
90	All I Ask of You (from *The Phantom of the Opera*)	Andrew Lloyd Webber/Charles Hart/Richard Stilgoe
126	All the Way	James Van Heusen/Sammy Cahn
6	Alleluja	Wolfgang Amadeus Mozart
81	And This Is My Beloved (from *Kismet*)	Robert Wright/George Forrest
158	Annie's Song	John Denver
14	Ave Maria	J.S. Bach/Charles Gounod
18	Ave Maria	Franz Schubert
22	Bist du bei mir (You Are with Me)	Gottfried Heinrich Stölzel – (previously attributed to J.S. Bach)
26	Dank sei Dir, Herr (Thanks Be to God)	Siegfried Ochs – (previously attributed to Handel)
168	Endless Love	Lionel Richie
31	Entreat Me Not to Leave Thee	Charles Gounod
129	Fly Me to the Moon	Bart Howard
100	The Greatest of These (from *Philemon*)	Harvey Schmidt/Tom Jones
176	Grow Old with Me	John Lennon
165	Here, There and Everywhere	John Lennon/Paul McCartney
204	How Beautiful	Twila Paris
132	I Could Write a Book	Richard Rodgers/Lorenz Hart
180	I Will	John Lennon/Paul McCartney
212	I Will Be Here	Steven Curtis Chapman
197	If You Could See What I See	Geoff Moore/Steven Curtis Chapman
183	In My Life	John Lennon/Paul McCartney
38	Jesu, Joy of Man's Desiring	J.S. Bach
135	Let It Be Me	Gilbert Becaud/Mann Curtis/Pierre DeLanoe
45	Let the bright Seraphim (from *Samson*)	George Frideric Handel
43	Let the bright Seraphim—trumpet part	
57	The Lord's Prayer	Albert Hay Malotte
218	Love of My Life	Jim Brickman/Tom Douglas

62	Mein gläubiges Herze (My Heart Ever Faithful)	J.S. Bach
95	More I Cannot Wish You (from *Guys and Dolls*)	Frank Loesser
236	My Place Is with You	Michael Puryear/Geoffrey Thurman
52	Now Thank We All Our God	arranged by Richard Walters
76	Panis Angelicus	César Franck
222	Parent's Prayer	Greg Davis
140	The Promise	David Shire/Alan and Marilyn Bergman
70	Pur ti miro, pur ti godo (from *L'incoronazione di Poppea*)	Claudio Monteverdi (realization by Richard Walters)
104	Some Enchanted Evening (from *South Pacific*)	Richard Rodgers/Oscar Hammerstein II
108	Someone Like You (from *Jekyll & Hyde*)	Frank Wildhorn/Leslie Bricusse
143	Starting Here, Starting Now	David Shire/Richard Maltby Jr.
112	Sunrise, Sunset (from *Fiddler on the Roof*)	Jerry Bock/Sheldon Harnick
226	This Day	Jadon Lavik
232	This Is the Day	Scott Wesley Brown
122	Till There Was You (from *The Music Man*)	Meredith Willson
146	Time After Time	Jule Styne/Sammy Cahn
117	Unexpected Song (from *Song & Dance*)	Andrew Lloyd Webber/Don Black
149	Walk Hand in Hand	Johnny Cowell
152	The Way You Look Tonight	Jerome Kern/Dorothy Fields
189	We've Only Just Begun	Roger Nichols/Paul Williams
155	With a Song in My Heart	Richard Rodgers/Lorenz Hart
186	You Are So Beautiful	Billy Preston/Bruce Fisher
192	You Raise Me Up	Brendan Graham/Rolf Lovland

Alleluja
from EXSULTATE, JUBILATE

Wolfgang Amadeus Mozart

Allegro non troppo (♩ = 116)

Al - le - lu - ja, al - le - lu - ja,_____ al - e - lu - ja, al - le - lu -

ja, al - le - lu - ja, al - le - lu - ja,_____

al - le - lu - ja, al - le - lu - ja,

al - le - lu - - ja, al - le -

lu - - ja,

al - - le - lu - ja, al - le - lu - ja,

al - le -

lu - ja, al - le - lu - ja, al - - - - - le - lu -

ja, _____

al - le - lu - - ja,

al - le - lu - ja, al -

le - lu - ja,

al - le - lu - ja, al - le - lu - ja, _____

al - le - lu -

ja, al - le - lu - ja, al - le - lu - ja,

cresc.

f

al - -

p

p

- - - - - - - -

p

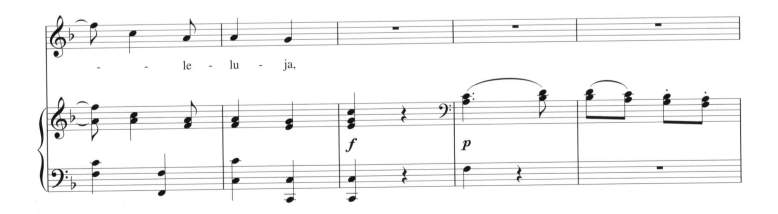

- - le - lu - ja,

al - le - lu - ja, al - le - lu -

ja,

al - le -

lu - ja, al - le - lu - ja, al - le -

lu - - - ja, al - le - lu - ja, al - le -

lu - ja, al - le - lu - ja,

al - le - lu - ja.

Ave Maria

Charles Gounod
adapted from the Prelude in C Major by J.S. Bach

Andante con moto

Do - mi - nus te - cum, be - ne -

dic - ta tu in mu - li -

e - ri-bus et _____ be - ne - dic - tus

fruc - tus _____ ven - tris _____

tu - i Je - sus. ____ Sanc - ta Ma-

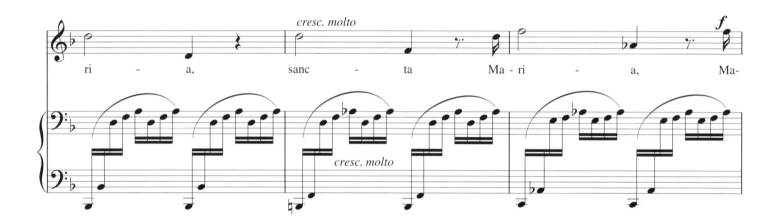

cresc. molto   *f*

ri - a,   sanc - ta Ma - ri - a,   Ma-

cresc. molto

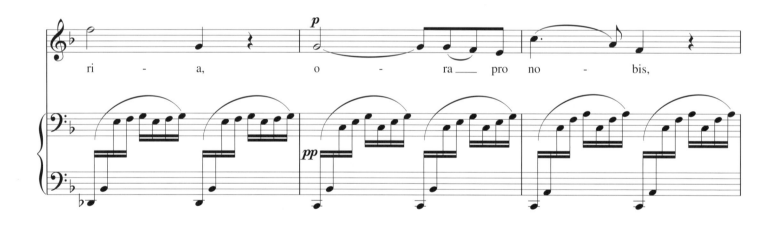

p

ri - a,   o - ra ____ pro no - bis,

pp

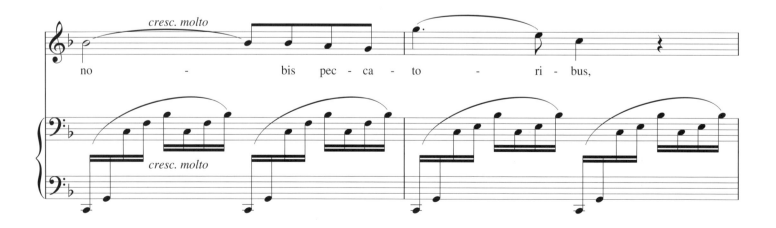

cresc. molto

no - bis pec - ca - to - ri - bus,

cresc. molto

nunc _____ et _____ in ho - ra, in

ho - ra _____ mor - tis _____ nos - trae, _____

A - men!

A - men!

Ave Maria

Franz Schubert

Sehr langsam (Molto adagio)

pp

(With pedal)

sim.

*A - - ve Ma - ri - -
A - - ve Ma - ri - -*

*a! gra - ti - a_____ ple -
a! Ma - ter_____ De -*

* Normally, at a wedding, only sing the first verse.

A - ve Ma - ri - -
A - ve Ma - ri - -

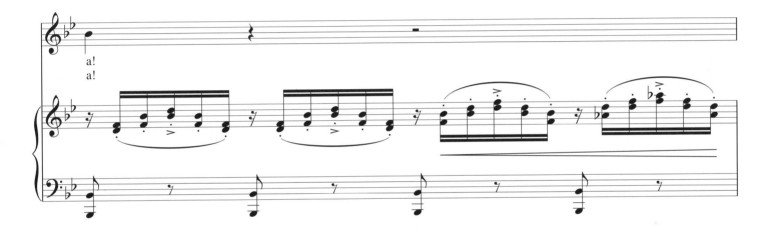

a!
a!

sim.

dim.

Bist du bei mir

(You Are with Me)

Gottfried Heinrich Stölzel
(previously attributed to J.S. Bach)

Anonymous

Bist du bei mir, geh' ich mit
You are with me, my joy for -

Freu - den zum Ster - ben__ und zu mei - ner__
ev - er. Un - til__ my__ death and un - to my

Ruh', zum__ Ster - ben und zu mei - ner Ruh'.
rest, un - til my death and un - to rest.

Bist du ___ bei ___ mir, geh' ich mit
You are ___ with ___ me, my joy for -

Freu - den zum Ster - ben ___ und zu mei - ner ___
ev - er. Un - til ___ my ___ death and un - to my

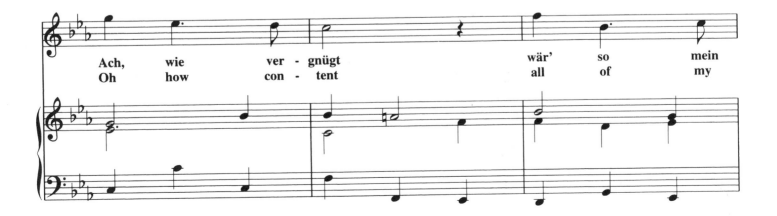

Ruh', zum ___ Ster - ben und zu mei - ner Ruh'.
rest, un - til ___ death and un - to rest.

Ach, wie ver - gnügt wär' so mein
Oh how con - tent all of my

En - de, Es drück - ten ___ dei - ne schö - nen ___
earth - ly days, And at ___ the ___ end will your ___ warm and

Hän - de mir ___ die ge - treu - en Au - gen zu.
lov - ing hand mir reach to ___ gent - ly ___ close my eyes.

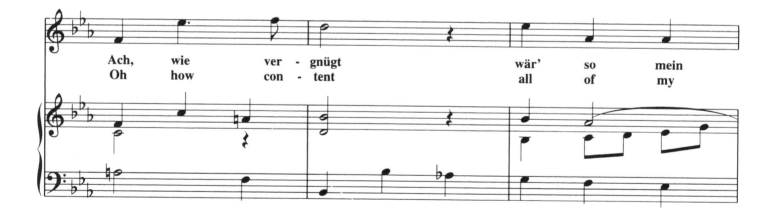

Ach, wie ver - gnügt wär' so mein
Oh how con - tent all of my

En - de, Es drück - ten ___ dei - ne schö - nen ___
days ___ And at ___ the ___ end will your ___ warm and

Hän - de mir ____ die ge - treu - en Au - gen zu.
lov - ing hand reach to ___ gent - ly ____ close my eyes.

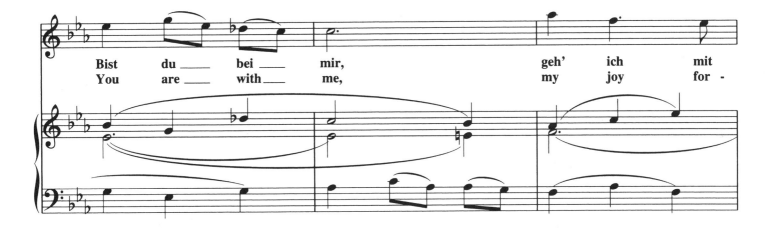

Bist du ____ bei ____ mir, geh' ich mit
You are ____ with ____ me, my joy for -

Freu - den, zum Ster - ben ____ und zu mei - ner ____
e - ver. Un - til ____ my ____ death and un - to my

Ruh'. zum _____ Ster - ben und zu mei - ner Ruh'.
rest, un - til ____ death and un - to rest.

Dank sei Dir, Herr
(Thanks Be to God)

Siegfried Ochs*
(previously attributed to Handel)

*Siegfried Ochs (1858-1929) claimed to have discovered an aria by Handel, and to have made an arrangement of the piece, which was published and became well-known. Closer research has revealed that this is actually an original composition by Ochs.

- ra - el hin durch das Meer.
grate - ful thanks be to Thee.

con espressione

f

sempre f

Wie ei - ne _____ Her - de zog _____ es hin - durch, _____
Like a _____ great _____ flock Thy hand _____ ev - er led _____ us,

Herr, _____ Dei - ne Hand Schütz - te es,
Lord _____ Thy _____ hand leads _____ us,

in Dei - ner _____ Gü - te gabst Du ihm Heil.
By all _____ Thy _____ good - ness Sal - va - tion is ours.

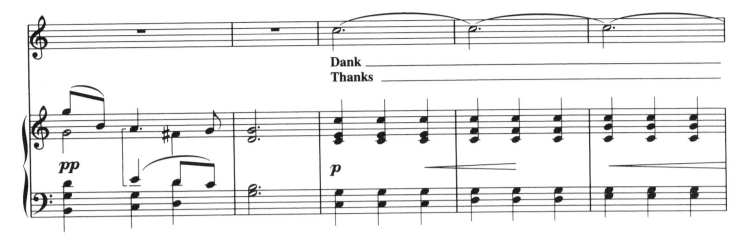

Dank _____
Thanks _____

__ sei Dir, { Dank _____ } sei Dir,
opt. { Herr, Dank _____
__ be to God, Thanks _____ be to

Herr,   Du   hast   Dein   Volk   mit   Dir   ge   führt,
God,   Thou who   has   made   thy   peo - ple   free,

Is -   ra - el   hin   durch   das   Meer.
All   grate - ful thanks be   to   Thee.
cresc.   con espressione

Entreat Me Not to Leave Thee
(Song of Ruth)

From the Book of Ruth 1:16-17

Charles Gounod

to re - turn from fol - low - ing af - ter thee, for

whith-er thou go - est I will go, and where thou lodg - est

I will lodge; whith-er thou go - est I___ will go, and

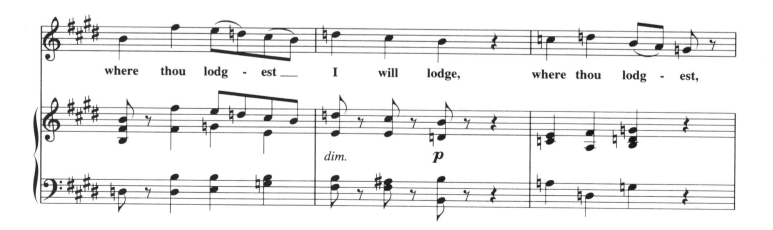

where thou lodg - est ___ I will lodge, where thou lodg - est,

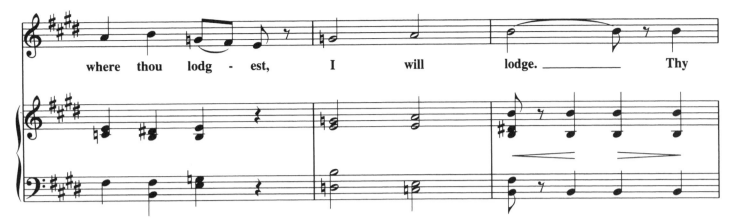

where thou lodg - est, I will lodge. _____ Thy

un poco meno presto, ma pochissimo

peo - ple shall be my peo - ple,

p

and thy __ God, my God; _____ thy

peo - ple shall be my peo - ple, and thy

God, _____ my God; _____ Thy

peo - ple shall be my peo - ple, and thy

God, my God. Where thou

di - est, will I die, _____ and there will I be

bur - ied; ___ The Lord do so to me, and more al - so, if aught but

death part thee and me, if aught but death __ part thee and

me. _____ Thy peo - ple shall be my

peo - ple, and thy ___ God, my

God;_____ Thy peo - ple shall be my

peo - ple, and thy God,_____ my

God;_____ Thy peo - ple shall be my

peo - ple, and thy God,_____ thy

God, my God.

Jesu, Joy of Man's Desiring

J.S. Bach
arranged by John Reed

Je - su, joy of man's de -
Through the way where hope is

sir - ing,
guid - ing,

Ho - ly wis - dom,
Hark, what peace - ful

Because of length, a singer may choose to perform just verse one.

Love ___ most ___ bright,
mu - sic ___ rings!

Drawn ___ by Thee, our souls ___ as - pir - ing
Where ___ the flock, in Thee ___ con - fid - ing,

Soar ___ to un - cre - at - ed ___
Drink ___ of joy from death - less ___

light.
springs.

Word of God, our flesh _____ that fash - ion'd
Theirs is beau - ty's fair - est pleas - ure,

mf

With the fire of
Theirs is wis - dom's

p   *cresc.*

life _____ im - pas - sion'd.
ho - liest treas - ure.

Striv - ing still to
Thou dost ev - er

Truth un - known,
lead un Thine own,

Soar - ing, dy - ing, round _____ Thy _____
In the love of joys _____ un -

42

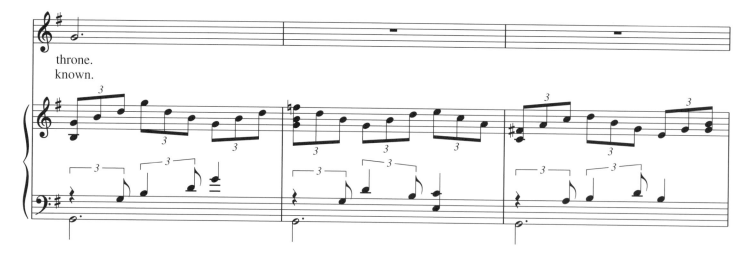

throne.
known.

Let the bright Seraphim
from SAMSON

George Frideric Handel

Fine   Da Capo al Fine

The part may be carefully cut from the book.

Let the bright Seraphim
from SAMSON

George Frideric Handel

AN ISRAELITE WOMAN:

Let the bright Se - ra-phim in

burn - ing row, their

*Play the small size notes in the absence of a trumpet.

46

loud, up - lift - ed an - gel trum - pets _ blow.

Let the bright Se - ra - phim in

burn - ing row, in burn - ing, burn - ing row, their

loud, up - lift - ed an - gel trum - pets blow, _____ their

loud, up - lift - ed an - gel trum - pets blow, _____

[cresc.]

[mf]

their loud, _____ their

[p]   [mf]

loud, up - lift - ed an - gel trum - pets blow,

[f]

let the bright Se - ra-phim in

[p]

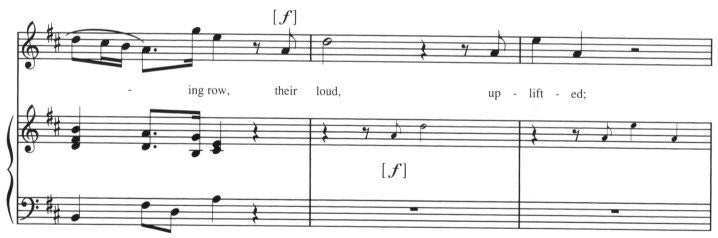

burn - ing row, in burn - ing, burn -

[mf]

[f]

- ing row, their loud, up - lift - ed;

[f]

an - gel _trum-pets blow, their loud, _____ up - lift - ed an - gel trum-pets blow, _____

their loud, _____ up - lift-ed an-gel

trum - pets blow.

[f]

Let the Che-ru - bic host, in

[p]

Fine

tune - ful choirs, touch their im - mor - tal harps _____ with gold - en wires,

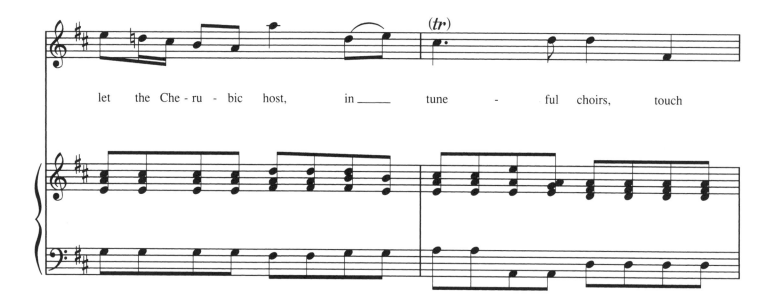

let the Che - ru - bic host, in _____ tune - ful choirs, touch

their im - mor - tal harps, touch their im - mor - tal harps _____

with gold - en

wires, _____ touch their im-mor-tal

harps ____ with gold - en wires.

[colla voce]   a tempo   [f]

Da Capo al Fine

for Gayletha

Now Thank We All Our God

Martin Rinckart, c. 1636
translated by Catherine Winkworth, 1858

"Nun danket alle Gott"
melody by Johann Crüger, 1648
altered by Felix Mendelssohn, 1840
arranged by Richard Walters

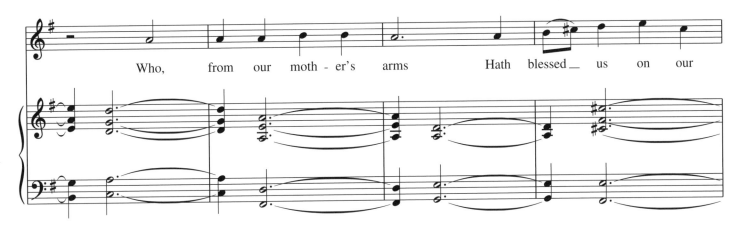

Who, from our moth-er's arms Hath blessed __ us on our

poco rit.

way With count-less gifts of love, And still is ours to-

a tempo

day.

a tempo

mp *espressivo* *mp*

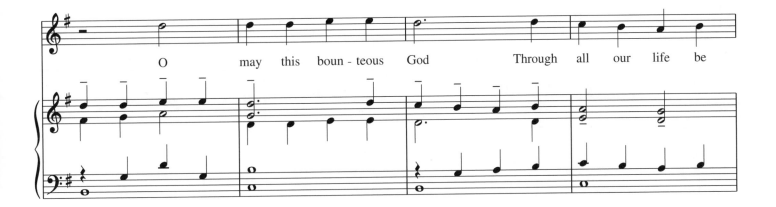

O may this boun-teous God Through all our life be

near us, With ev - er joy - ful

hearts And bless - ed peace to cheer us, And

keep us in his grace, And guide __ us when per -

plexed, And free us from all

ills In this world and the next.

All praise and thanks to God The

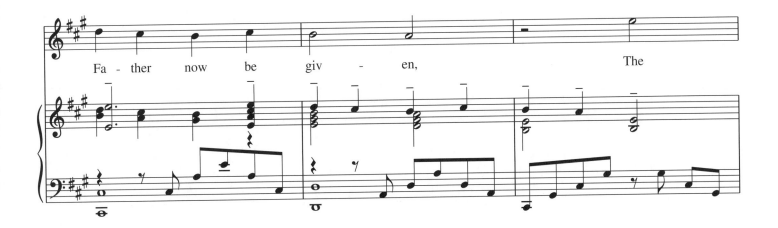

Fa - ther now be giv - en, The

Son, and him who reigns with them in high-est heav - en,

The one e - ter - nal God, Whom

earth __ and heav'n a - dore For

thus it was, is now, And shall be __ ev - er more.

gratefully dedicated to my friend John Charles Thomas

The Lord's Prayer

Albert Hay Malotte

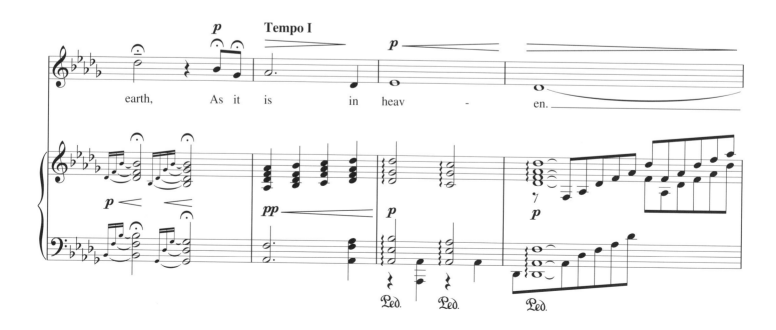

L'istesso tempo

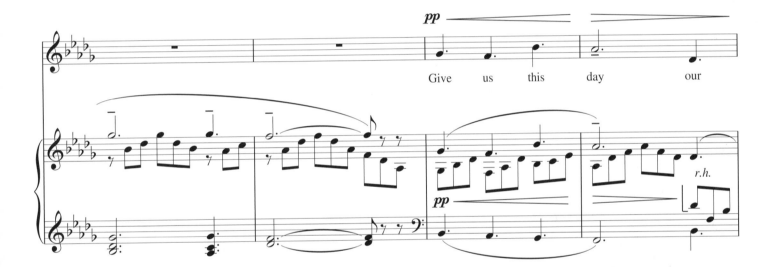

Give us this day our

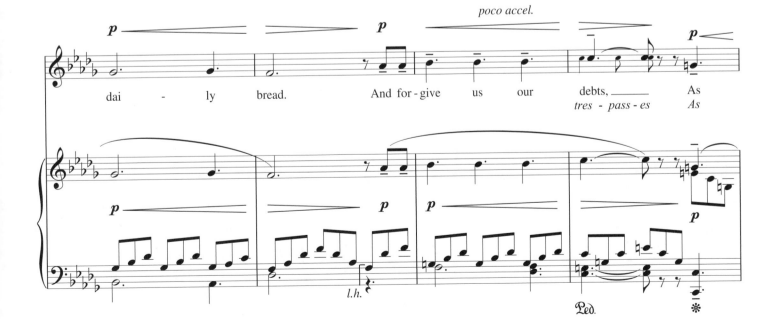

dai - ly bread. And for-give us our debts, _____ As
tres - pass - es As

we _____ for-give our debt - ors.
we for-give those who tres-pass a - gainst us.

And lead us not in - to temp - ta - tion; But de - liv - er us from

Poco meno mosso, e sonoramente

e - vil: For thine is the king - dom, _____ and the

Mein gläubiges Herze
(My Heart Ever Faithful)
from CANTATA No. 68

J.S. Bach

lok - ke, _____ sing', scher - ze, dein Je - sus _____ ist nah!
prais - es, be joy - ful, thy Je - sus is near!

Weg Jam - mer, weg Kla - gen, weg
A - way _____ with com - plain - ing, a -

Jam - mer, weg Kla - gen, ich will _____ euch nur sa - gen: mein
way _____ with com - plain - ing, Faith ev - er main - tain - ing, My

Je - sus ist da; weg Jam - mer, weg Kla - gen, ich
Je - sus is here; *A - way___ with com - plain - ing, Faith*

will___ euch nur sa - gen: mein Je - sus___ ist nah', mein___
ev - er main - tain - ing, My Je - sus is here, my___

Je - sus___ ist da,
Je - sus is here;

Weg
A -

Jam - mer, weg Kla - gen, weg Jam - mer, weg Kla - gen, ich
way___ with com - plain - ing, a - way___ with com - plain - ing, Faith

will___ euch nur sa - gen:___ mein Je - sus___ ist da. Mein
ev - er main - tain - ing, My Je - sus is here. My

gläu - bi - ges Her - ze, froh - lok - ke,_____ sing', scher - ze,
heart _____ ev - er faith - ful, sing prais - es, be joy - ful,

mein
My

p

gläu - bi - ges Her - ze, froh - lok - ke,_____ sing', scher - ze, froh -
heart _____ ev - er faith - ful, sing prais - es, be joy - ful, sing

lok - ke,_____ sing', scher - ze,_____ dein Je - sus ist nah, froh -
prais - es, be joy - ful, thy Je - sus is near sing

lok - ke, sing', scher - ze, froh - lok -
prais - es, be joy - ful, sing prais -

- ke,_____ sing', scher - ze, mein
- es,_____ be joy - ful, my

gläu - bi - ges Her - ze, froh - lok - ke, _____ sing', scher - ze, froh -
heart _____ ev - er faith - ful, sing prais - es, be joy - ful, sing

lok - ke, _____ sing', scher - ze, dein Je - sus _____ ist nah!
prais - es, be joy - ful, thy Je - sus is near!

Pur ti miro, pur ti godo

from *L'incoronazione di Poppea*

Claudio Monteverdi
realization by Richard Walters

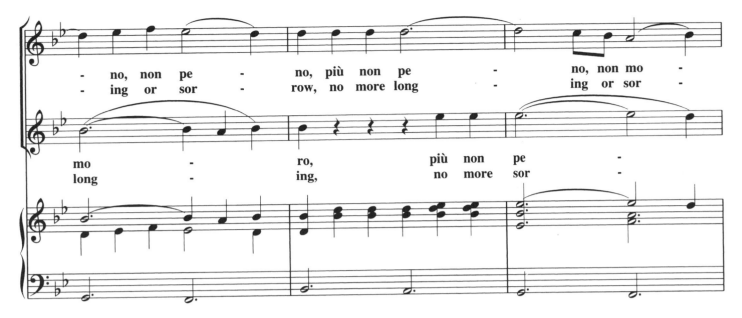

72

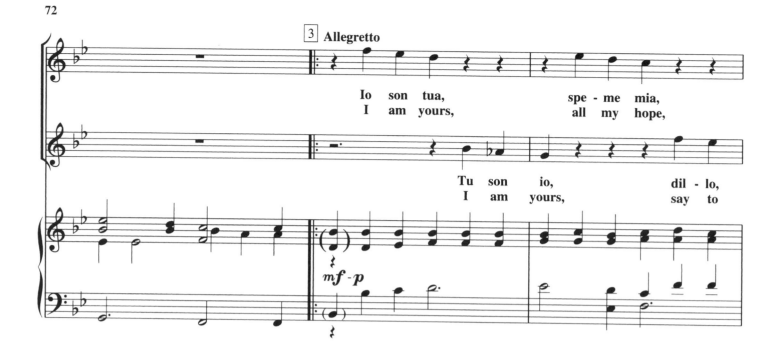

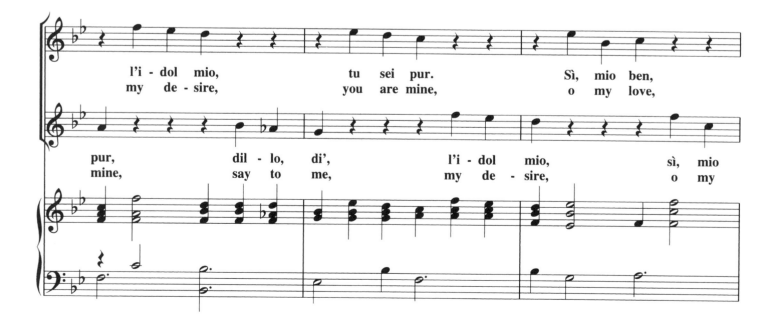

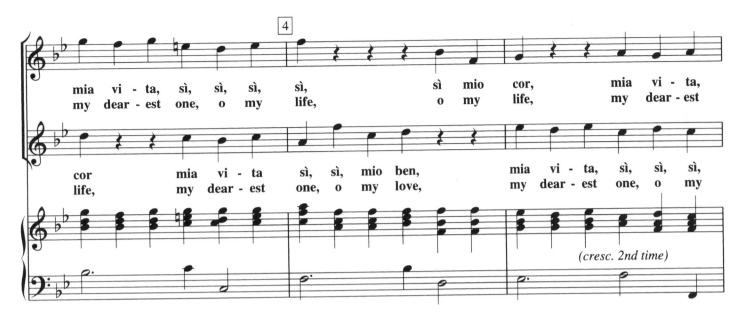

74

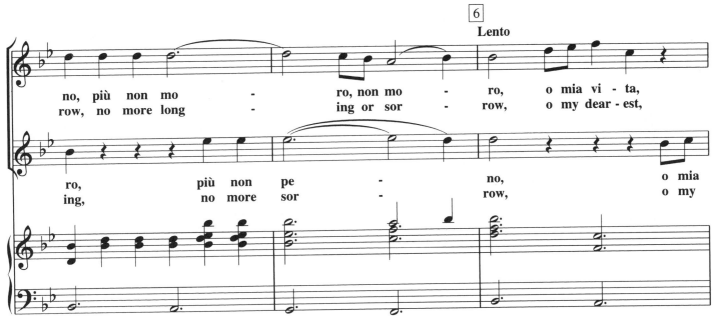

Panis Angelicus

César Franck

ge - li - cus   fit   pa - nis   ho - mi - num,

Dat   pa - nis   coe - li - cus   fi - gu - ris ter - mi -

num.   O   res   mi - ra - bi - lis

man - du - cat   Do - mi - num,   Pau - per,

pau - per, ser - vus et hu - mi - lis,

Pau - per, pau - per, ser - vus et hu - mi -

lis.

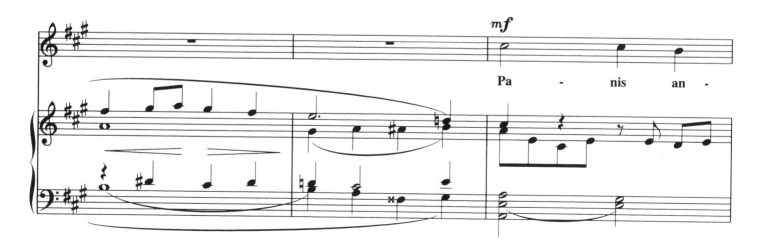

Pa - nis an -

ge - li -cus   fit   pa - nis   ho - mi -num,

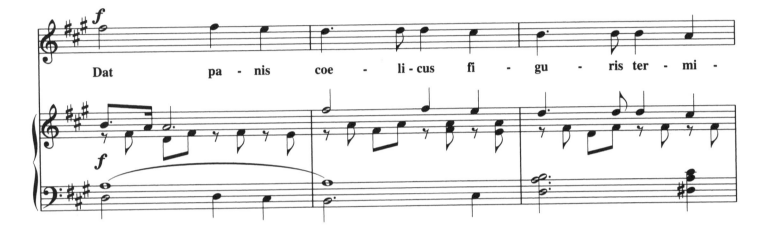

Dat   pa - nis   coe - li -cus   fi - gu - ris ter - mi -

num.   O   res   mi - ra bi - lis,

man - du - cat   Do - mi -num   Pau -   per, —

pau - per, ser - vus et hu - mi - lis,

Pau - per, — pau - per, ser - vus, — ser - vus et

hu - mi - lis.

And This Is My Beloved
from KISMET

Words and Music by
Robert Wright and George Forrest
(Music based on themes of A. Borodin)

Andantino

Dawn's prom-is-ing skies, Pet-als on a pool drift - ing; I -

mag-ine these _____ in one pair of eyes, And this is my be - lov - ed.

Strange spice from the south, Hon-ey through the comb

sift - ing; I - mag - ine these _____ on one ea - ger mouth,

Poco più mosso

And this is my be - lov - ed. And when he speaks,

And when he talks to me, Mu - sic! Mys - ter - y!

And when he moves And when he walks with me, Par - a - dise _____ comes sud - den - ly

All Good Gifts
from the Musical GODSPELL

Words and Music by
Stephen Schwartz

Moderately (♩ = 68)

We plow the fields,— and scat- ter the good seed on— the

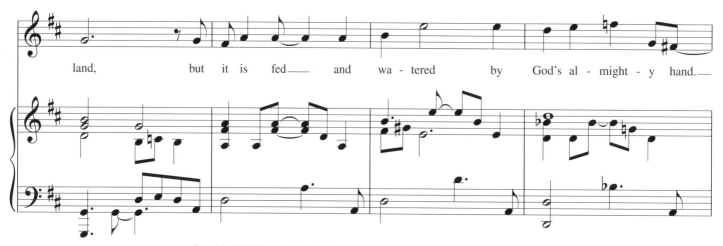

land, but it is fed— and wa- tered by God's al- might- y hand.—

He sends the snow_____ in win - ter, the

warmth to swell____ the grain, the breez - es and____ the sun - shine, and

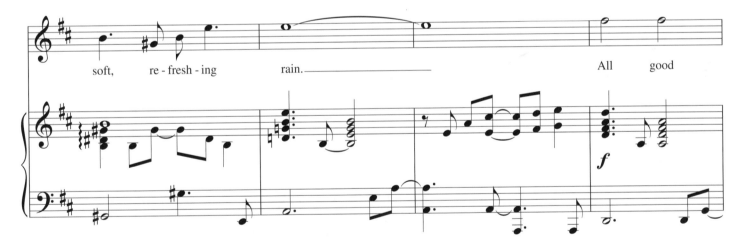

soft, re - fresh - ing rain._____ All good

gifts a - round____ us_____ are sent from

heav - en a - bove._____ Then thank the

Lord, O, thank_____ the Lord for all his love._____

We

thank thee, then O Fa-ther, for all things bright and good, the

seed time and the har - vest, our life, our health, our

food. No gifts have we to of - fer for all thy love im -

parts, but that which thou de - sir - est, our

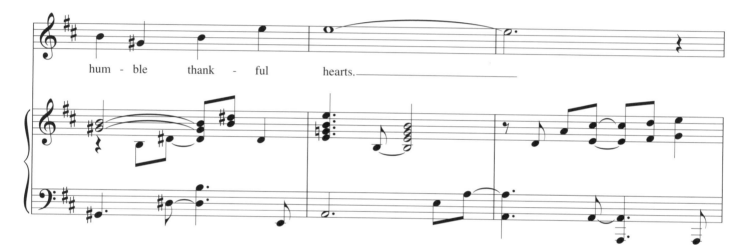

hum - ble thank - ful hearts._____

All good gifts a - round_____ us_____

are sent from heav - en a - bove._____

So thank the Lord, O, thank

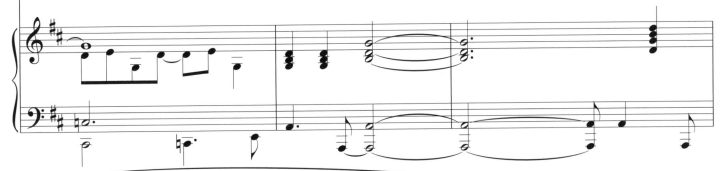

the Lord for all his love.

f

I thank you Lord,

ff   *molto rit.*

All I Ask of You
from THE PHANTOM OF THE OPERA

Music by Andrew Lloyd Webber
Lyrics by Charles Hart
Additional Lyrics by Richard Stilgoe

here, with you, be-side you, to guard you and to guide you.

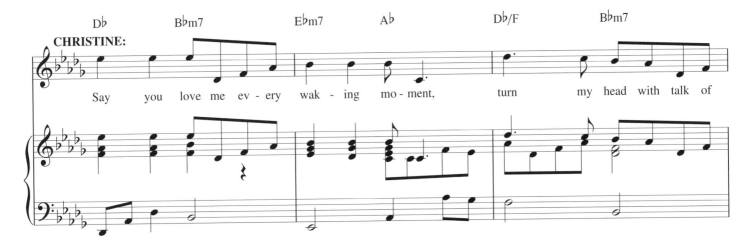

CHRISTINE:
Say you love me ev-ery wak-ing mo-ment, turn my head with talk of

sum-mer-time. Say you need me with you now and al-ways;

pro-mise me that all you say is true, that's all I ask of

Let me be your shel-ter, let me be your light; you're safe, no one will find you your
you.

fears are far be-hind you. All I want is free-dom, a world with no more night; and

you, al-ways be-side me, to hold me and to hide me. Then say you'll share with me one

love, one life-time; let me lead you from your sol-i-tude. __

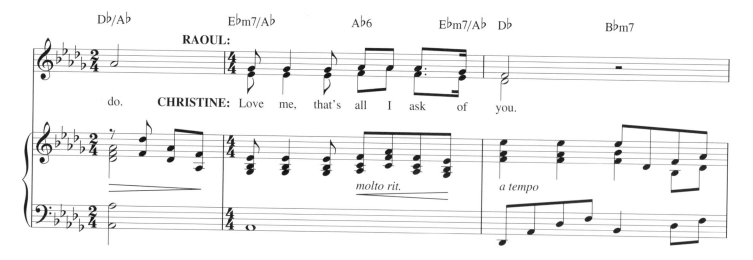

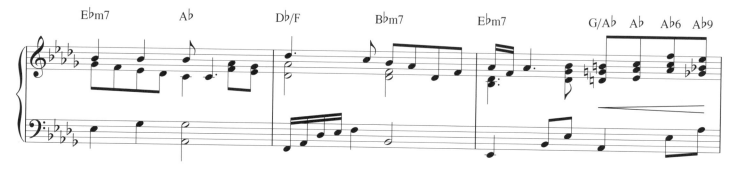

More I Cannot Wish You
from GUYS AND DOLLS

By Frank Loesser

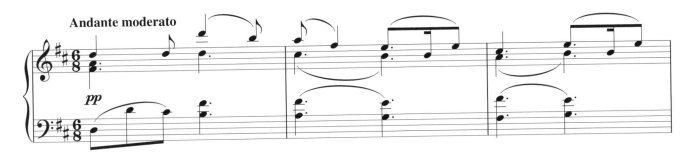

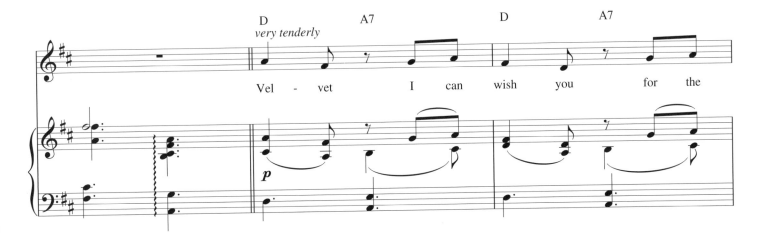

96

wish you find your love, _____ Your own true love, _____ this

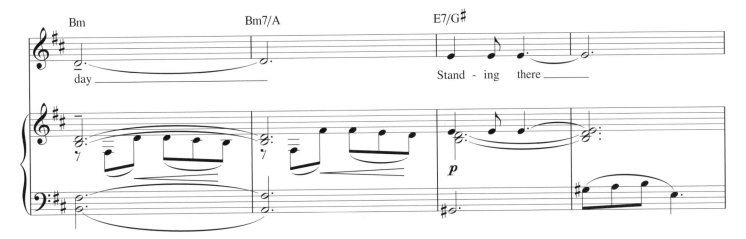

day _____ Stand - ing there _____

Gaz - ing at you _____ Full _____ of the bloom _____ of

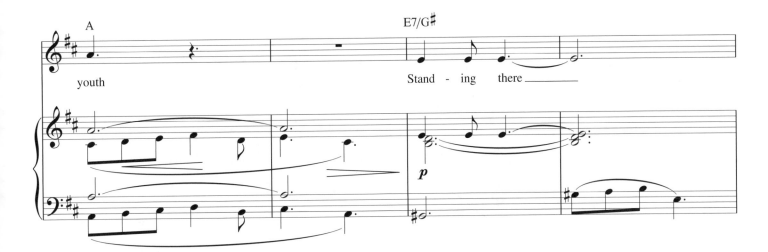

youth Stand - ing there _____

Gaz - ing at you _____ With the sheep's eye _____ And the

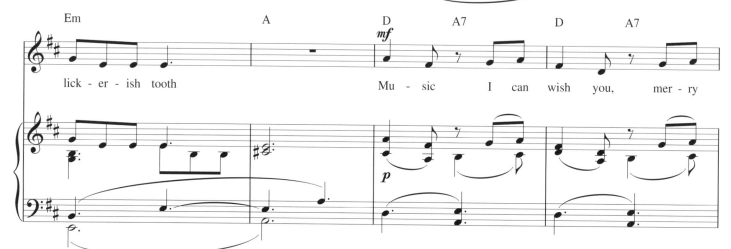

lick - er - ish tooth Mu - sic I can wish you, mer - ry

mu - sic while you're young, _____ And wis - dom, when your hair has turned to

gray _____ But more I can - not wish ___ you than to

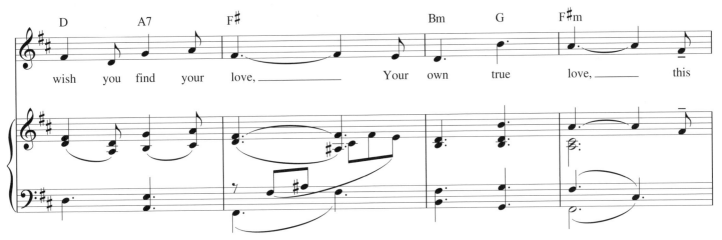

wish you find your love, _____ Your own true love, _____ this

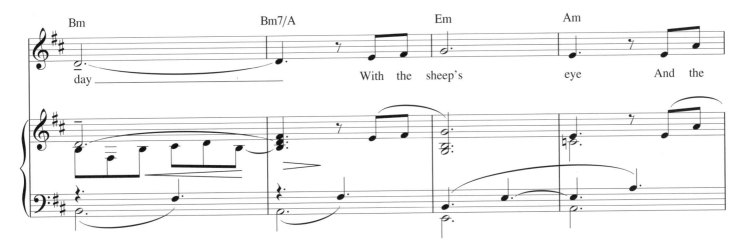

day _____ With the sheep's eye And the

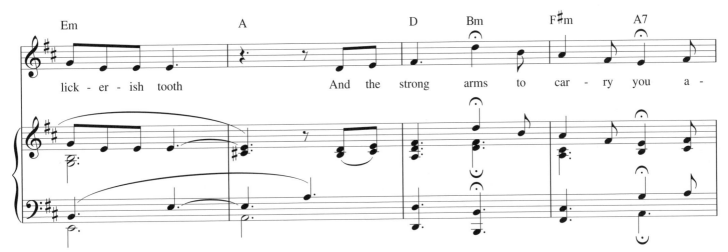

lick - er - ish tooth And the strong arms to car - ry you a -

way. _____

The Greatest of These

from PHILEMON

Words and Music by Tom Jones
and Harvey Schmidt

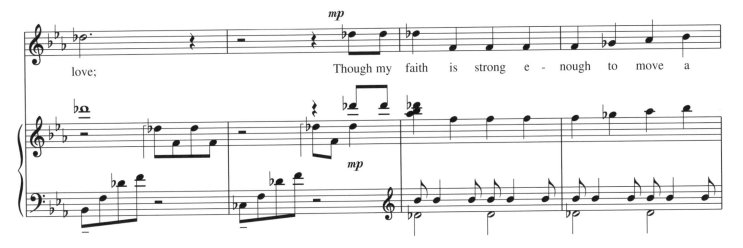

love; Though my faith is strong e - nough to move a

moun - tain. Though I be - stow my world - ly goods to feed the

poor. Though my bod - y may be

tor - tured, if I have not lived with love I am

noth-ing but a sound-ing brass a tin-kling cym-bal, noth-ing,

noth-ing. But with love, I can bear it all re -

joic - ing, be - cause of love be - cause of

love._____ For love suf - fers ev - 'ry-thing

love bear - eth ev - 'ry-thing! Love hop - eth

Broader

ev - 'ry-thing! Love be - liev - eth ev - 'ry-thing! There a -

bid - eth three things: Faith, hope and love. But the

great - est of these is love

Some Enchanted Evening

from SOUTH PACIFIC

Lyrics by Oscar Hammerstein II
Music by Richard Rodgers

Someone Like You
from JEKYLL & HYDE

Words by Leslie Bricusse
Music by Frank Wildhorn

Slowly, with expression

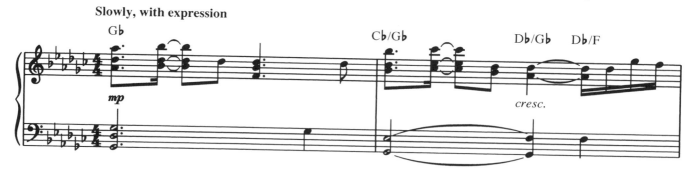

I peered through win-dows, watched life go by. Dreamed of to-mor-row,
It's like you took my dreams, made each one real. You reached in-side of me

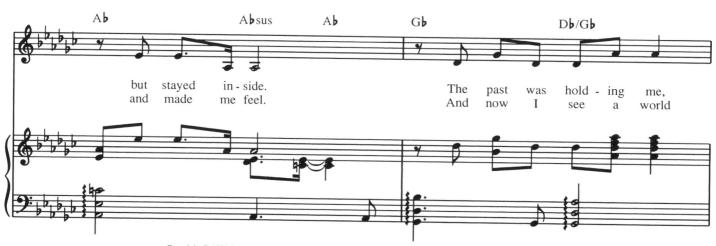

but stayed in - side. The past was hold - ing me,
and made me feel. And now I see a world

keep-ing life at bay.
I've nev-er seen be-fore.

I wan-dered, lost in yes-ter-
Your love has o-pened ev-'ry

cresc.

To Coda ⊕

day, want-ing to fly, but scared to try. Then
door. You've set me

some-one like you found some-one like me, and

sud-den - ly _____ noth-ing is the same. My

dim.

heart's tak - en wing, ___ and I feel so a - live, ___ 'cause

D.S. al Coda

some-one like you found me.

CODA

free, now I can soar for

some - one like you found some - one like me, and

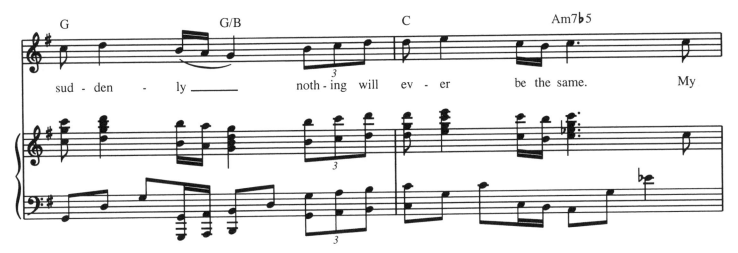

sud - den - ly _____ noth - ing will ev - er be the same. My

heart's tak - en wing, _____ and I feel so a - live, _____ 'cause

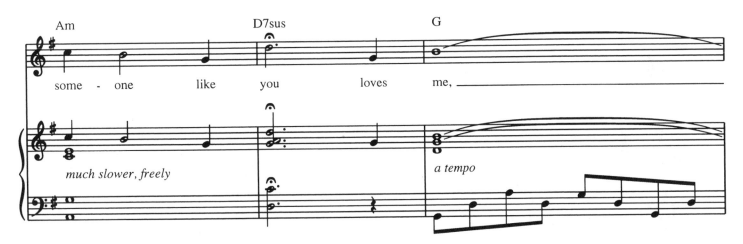

some - one like you loves me, _____

Sunrise, Sunset
from the Musical FIDDLER ON THE ROOF

Words by Sheldon Harnick
Music by Jerry Bock

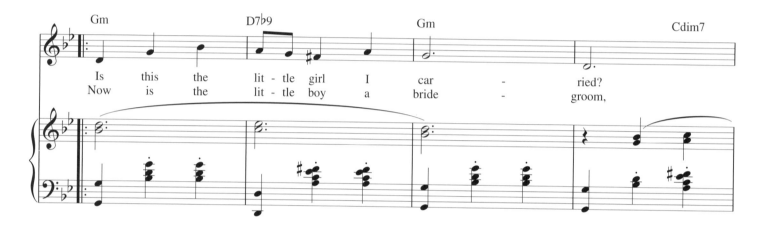

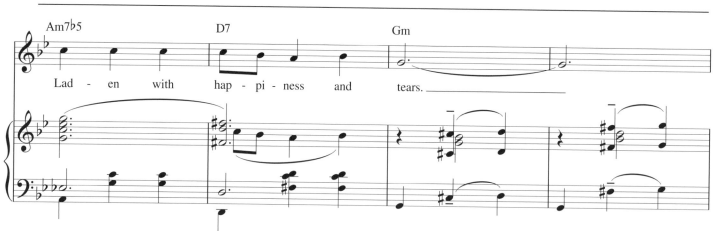

Lad - en with hap - pi - ness and tears. _____

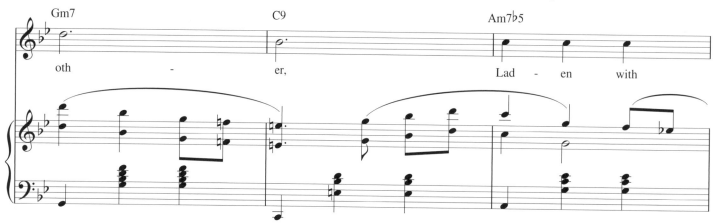

One sea - son fol - low - ing an -

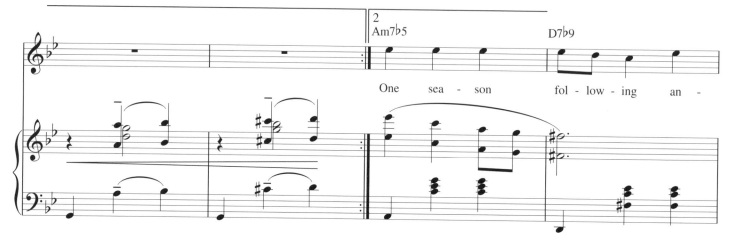

oth - er, Lad - en with

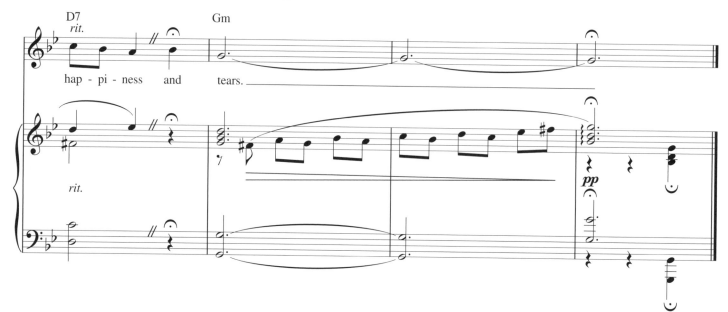

hap - pi - ness and tears. _____

Unexpected Song
from SONG & DANCE

Music by Andrew Lloyd Webber
Lyrics by Don Black

know the kind of love you've shown me. }
though you could-n't bear to lose me. }

Now no mat-ter where I am, no mat-ter what I

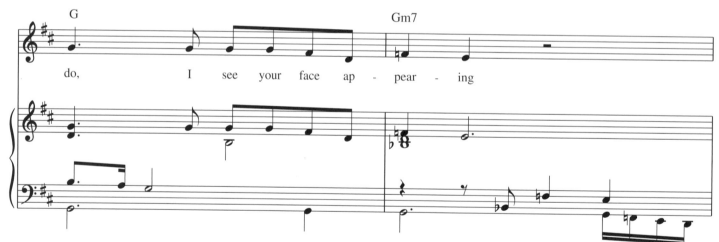

do, I see your face ap - pear - ing

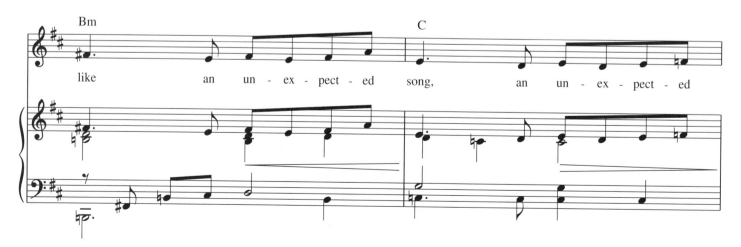

like an un-ex-pect-ed song, an un-ex-pect-ed

song that on-ly we are hear - ing.   hear - ing.

I   have nev - er felt like   this.   For once I'm lost for

words,   your smile has real - ly   thrown me.

This   is   not like me at   all;   I nev - er thought I'd

120

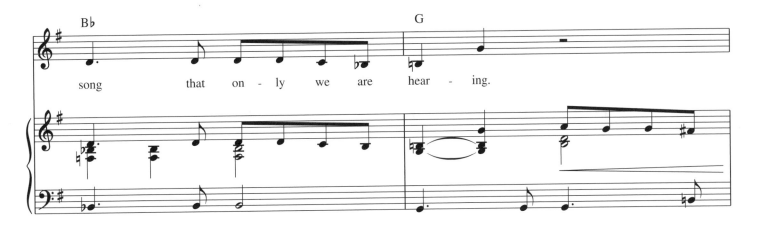

song that on - ly we are hear - ing.

Like an un - ex - pect - ed song, an un - ex - pect - ed

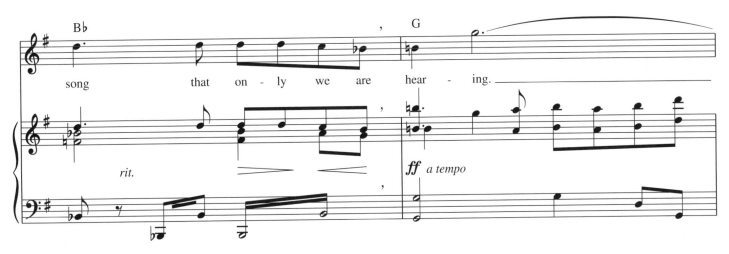

song that on - ly we are hear - ing.

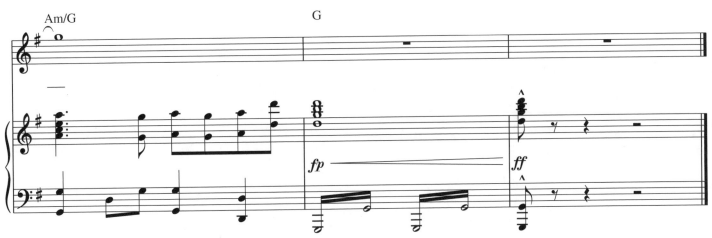

Till There Was You

from Meredith Willson's THE MUSIC MAN

By Meredith Willson

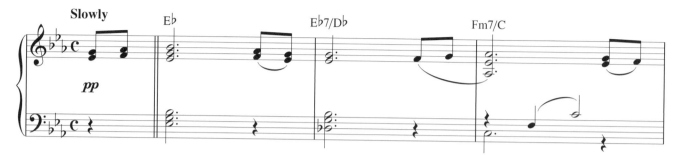

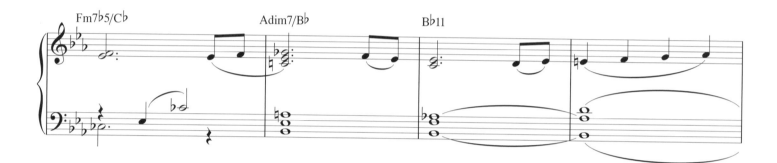

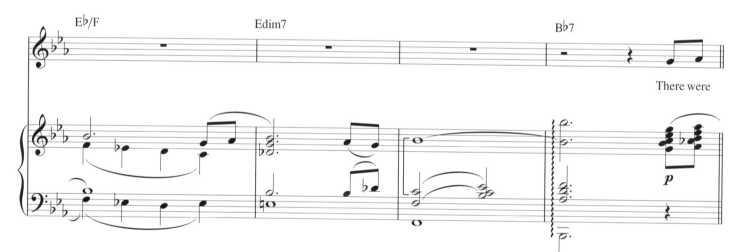

nev - er heard them at all, till there was you._____ There were

birds in the sky, but I nev - er saw them wing - ing. No I

nev - er saw them at all, till there was you._____ And there was

mu - sic and there were won - der - ful ro - ses, they tell me, in

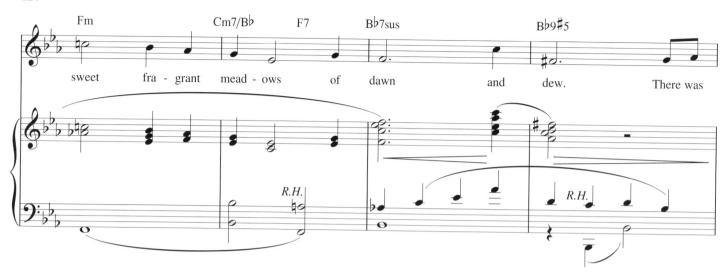

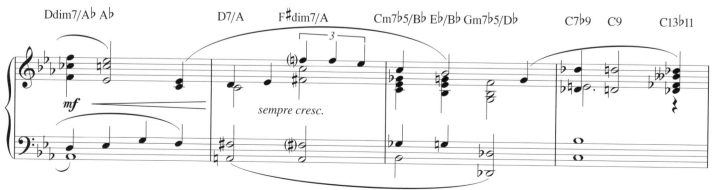

There was

love all a-round, but I nev-er heard it sing-ing. No, I

nev-er heard it at all, till there was you.

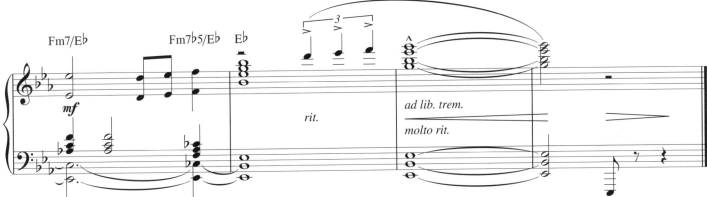

All the Way

from the film THE JOKER IS WILD

Words by Sammy Cahn
Music by James Van Heusen
arranged by Hank Powell

Slowly, with rubato

way.

Tall - er _____ than the tall - est tree is, that's how it's got to

cresc. *mf*

feel.

Deep - er _____ than the deep blue sea is, that's how deep it goes, __ if it's

real.

When some-bod - y needs you, it's no good un-less { he / she } needs you

decresc. poco rit. *a tempo* *mp*

all the way.

Through the good or lean years and for

p *cresc.*

all the in - be - tween years, come what may.

Who knows _____ where the road will lead us, on - ly a fool would say. But

if you let me love you, it's for sure I'm gon - na love you all the way,

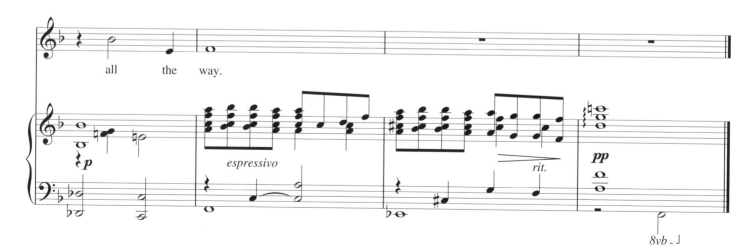

all the way.

8vb

Fly Me to the Moon
(In Other Words)

Words and Music by
Bart Howard
arranged by Hank Powell

Gently, slowly

Fly me to the moon, and let me play a - mong the stars;

Let me see what spring is like on Ju - pit - er and Mars. In

oth - er words: _____ hold my hand. In oth - er words: _____

130

dar - ling, kiss me. _____ Fill my heart with

song, and let me sing for - ev - er - more. You are all I

long for, all I wor - ship and a - dore. In oth - er words: _____ please be

true. _____ In oth - er words: I love you.

You are all I long for, all I wor - ship and a - dore. In

oth - er words: _____ please be true. _____ In oth - er words:

I love you. _____

I Could Write a Book

from PAL JOEY

Words by Lorenz Hart
Music by Richard Rodgers
Arranged by Brian Dean

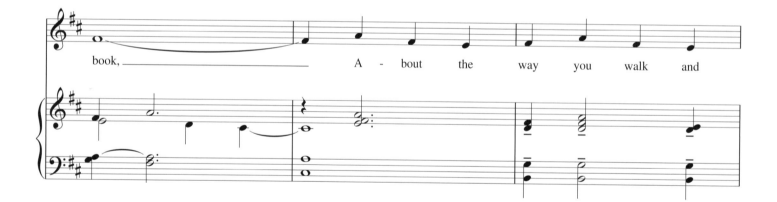

lot. _____ Then the world dis -

cov - ers as my book ends, how to make two

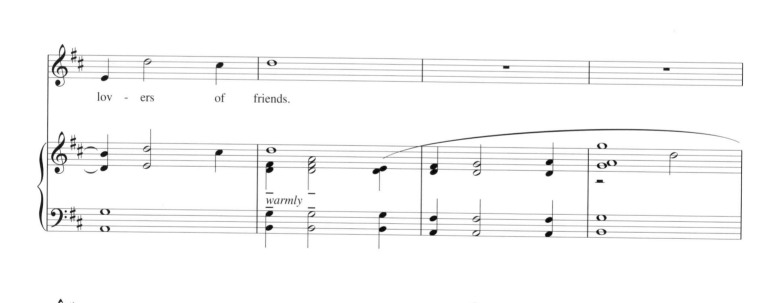

lov - ers of friends.

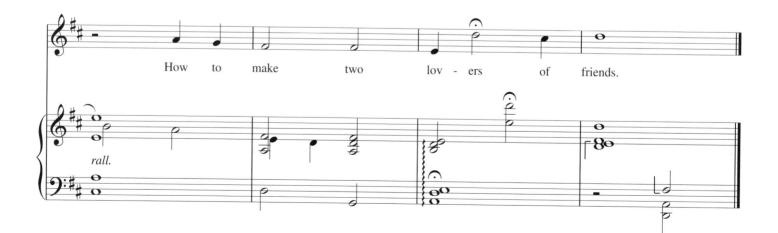

How to make two lov - ers of friends.

Let It Be Me
(Je T'appartiens)

English Words by Mann Curtis
French Words by Pierre DeLanoe
Music by Gilbert Becaud
Arranged by John Reed

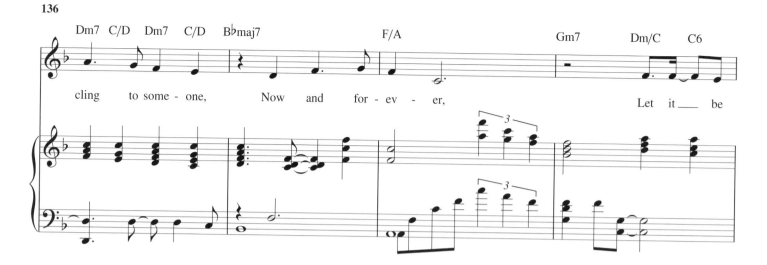

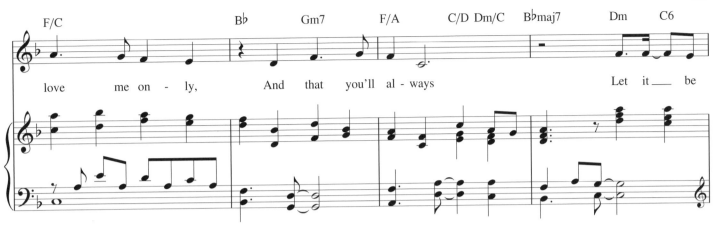

love me on - ly, And that you'll al - ways

Let it ___ be

me.

If, for each bit of glad - ness, Some - one must

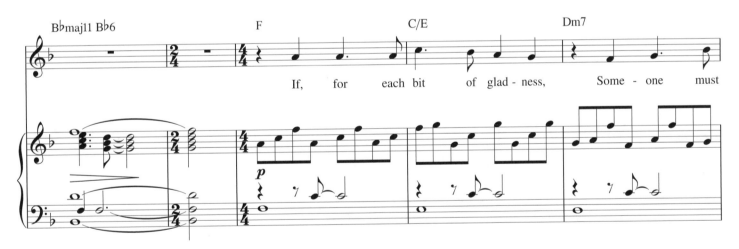

taste of sad - ness, I'll bear the sor - row,

Let it be

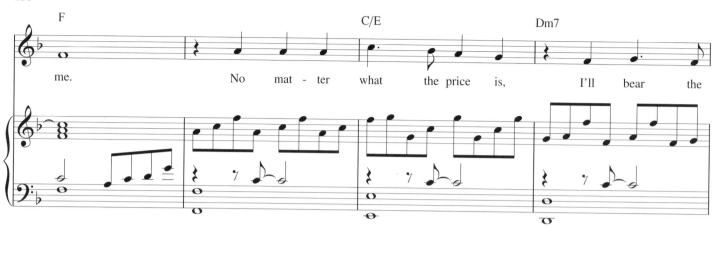

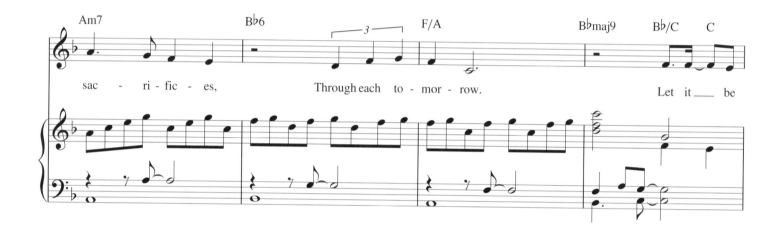

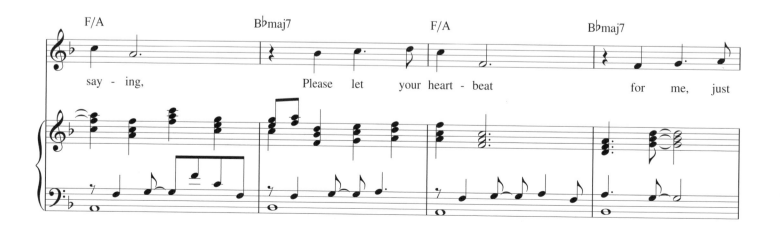

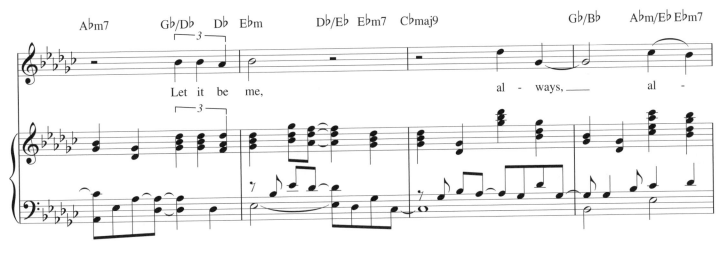

The Promise
(I'll Never Say Goodbye)
Theme from the Universal Motion Picture THE PROMISE

Words by Alan and Marilyn Bergman
Music by David Shire

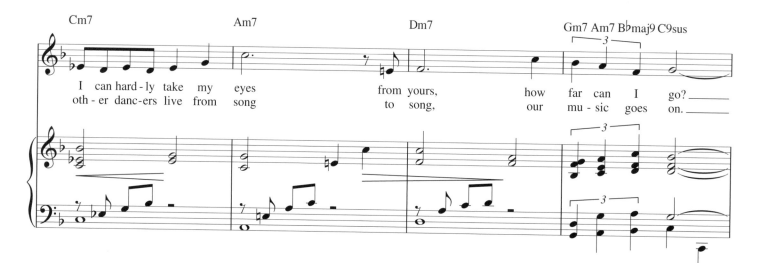

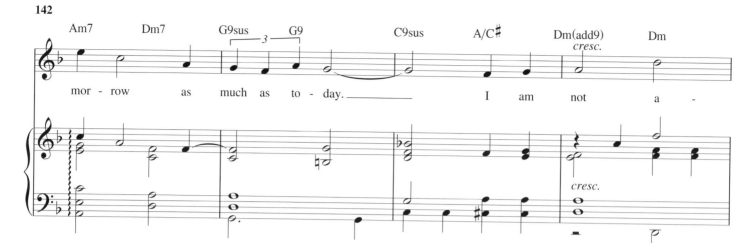

mor - row   as   much   as   to - day. _____   I am   not   a -

fraid to say,   "I love   you," _____   and I prom - ise you I'll

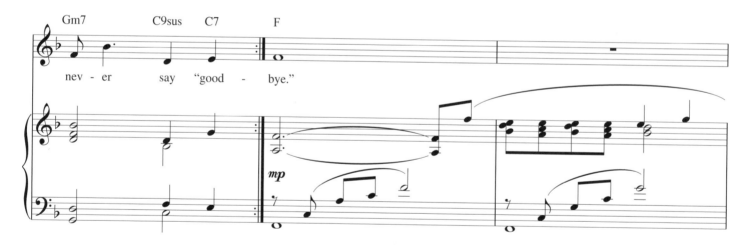

nev - er   say   "good - bye."

How   could I ev - er say "good - bye?"

*Cue notes optional 2nd time

Starting Here, Starting Now

Words by Richard Maltby Jr.
Music by David Shire

144

Time After Time

from the Metro-Goldwyn-Mayer Picture IT HAPPENED IN BROOKLYN

Words by Sammy Cahn
Music by Jule Styne
Arranged by Richard Walters

I on-ly know what I know, the pass-ing years will show you've

kept my love so young, so new. _____ And time af-ter

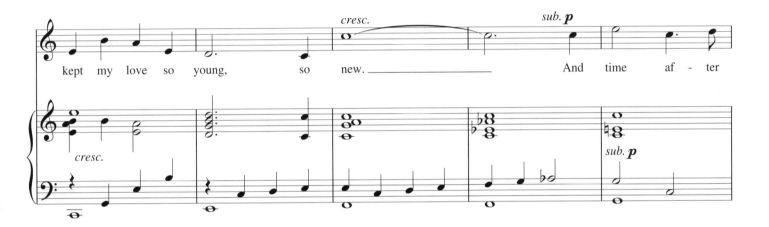

time, you'll hear me say that I'm so luck-y to be

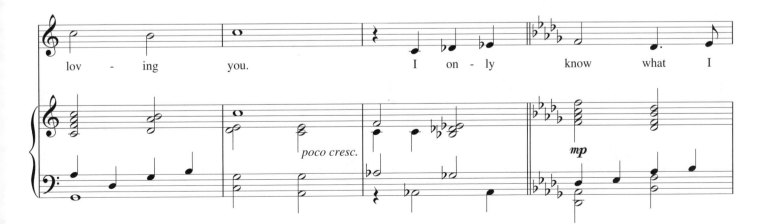

lov-ing you. I on-ly know what I

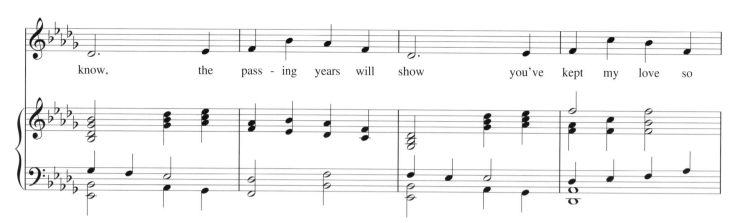

know, the pass - ing years will show you've kept my love so

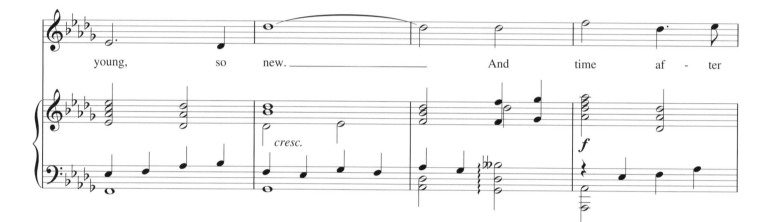

young, so new. And time af - ter

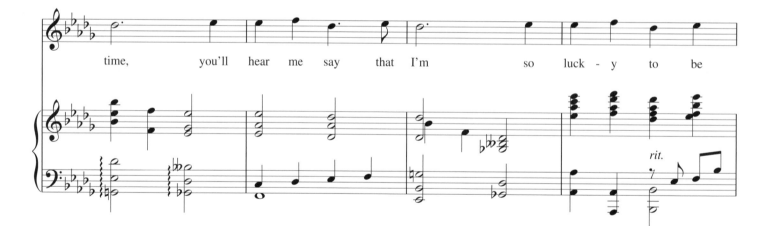

time, you'll hear me say that I'm so luck - y to be

lov - ing you.

Walk Hand in Hand

Words and Music by
Johnny Cowell
Arranged by Joel K. Boyd

Walk hand in hand with me through all e-

ter - ni - ty, have faith, be - lieve in me,

give me your hand. Love is a

150

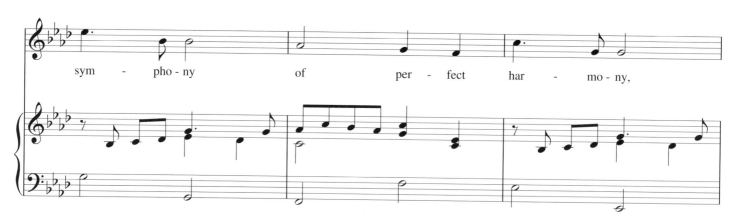

sym - pho - ny   of   per - fect   har - mo - ny,

when   lov - ers   such   as   we   walk   hand   in

hand.   Be   not   a - fraid,   for

I   am with you all the while.   So   lift _____ your head up

high _____ and look _____ to - ward the sky!

Walk hand in hand with me, God is our

des - ti - ny, no great - er love could be, walk hand in

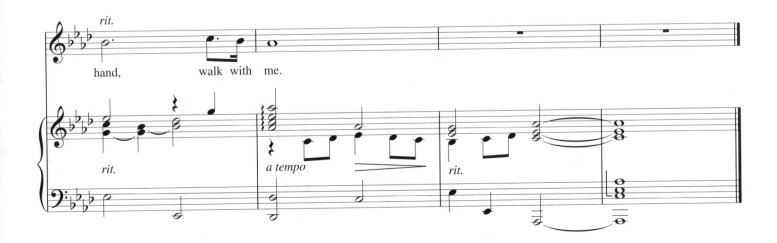

hand, walk with me.

The Way You Look Tonight

from the film SWING TIME

Words by Dorothy Fields
Music by Jerome Kern
Arranged by Hank Powell

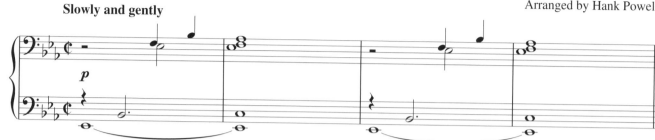

night.   With   each   word   your

ten - der - ness   grows, ___   tear - ing   my   fear _____   a -

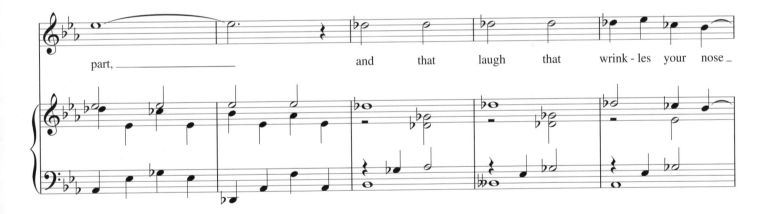

part, _____   and   that   laugh   that   wrink - les   your   nose __

touch - es   my   fool - ish   heart. _____

poco cresc.

Love - ly, nev - er, nev - er change, keep that breath-less

charm, won't you please ar - range it, 'cause I love you

just the way you look to - night, _____ just the way you

look to - night. _____

With a Song in My Heart

from SPRING IS HERE

Words by Lorenz Hart
Music by Richard Rodgers
Arranged by Richard Walters

hand; It tells that you're stand - ing near,

and At the sound of your voice Heav-en o - pens its

por - tals to me. Can I help but re - joice

That a song such as ours came to be? But I al - ways knew _____

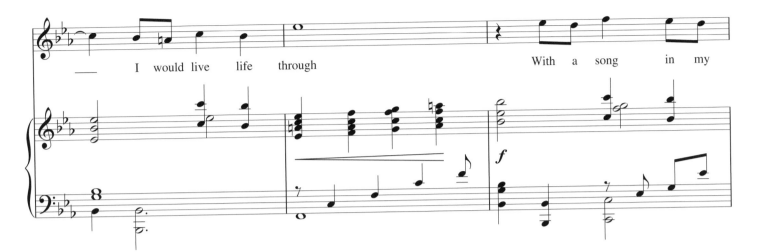

I would live life through

With a song in my

heart for you.

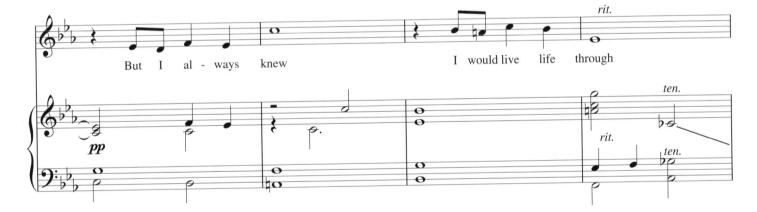

But I al - ways knew

I would live life through

Slowly to the end

With a song in my heart for you.

Annie's Song
Recorded by John Denver

Words and Music by John Denver
Arranged by Richard Walters

Moderately fast; flowing

spring - time, _____ like a walk in the rain,

_____ Like a storm in the __

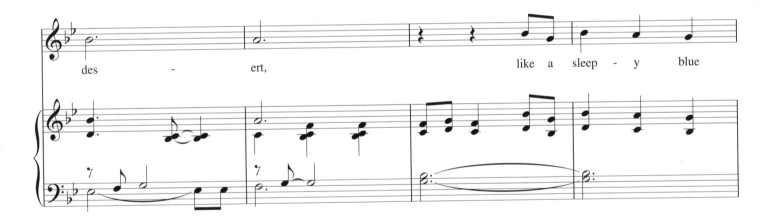

des - ert, like a sleep - y blue

o - cean, _____ You fill up my __

sen - - ses, come fill me a -

gain.

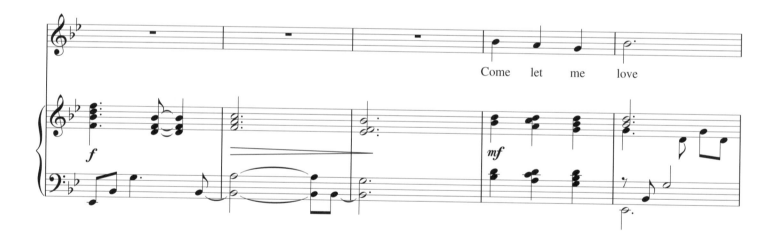

Come let me love

you, let me give my life to

you, _____ Let me drown in your laugh -

ter, let me die in your arms, _____

Let me

lay down be - side _____ you, _____ let me

al - ways be with you, _____ come _

_ let me love _____ you, come

love me a - gain. _____

You fill up my sen - ses

like a night in a for - est, like the

moun - tains in spring - time, like a walk in the

rain, like a storm in the des -

ert, like a sleep - y blue o - cean, __

you fill up my sen - ses, *rit.*

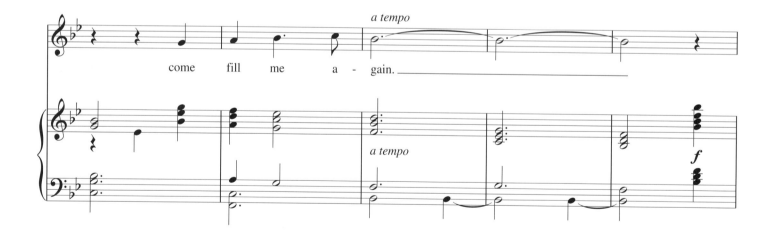

come fill me a - gain. _____ *a tempo*

Here, There and Everywhere

Recorded by The Beatles

Words and Music by John Lennon
and Paul McCartney

Endless Love
Recorded by Lionel Richie

Words and Music by
Lionel Richie

Moderately slow

step I make. ___ And I,

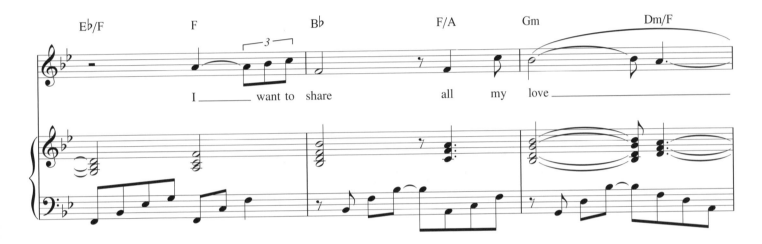

I _____ want to share all my love _____

___ with you, no one else _____ will ___ do. ___

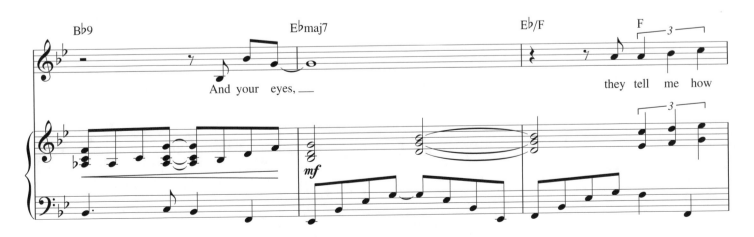

And your eyes, ___ they tell me how

beat as __ one; __ our lives have just be - gun. __

For - ev - er, __ I'll hold you

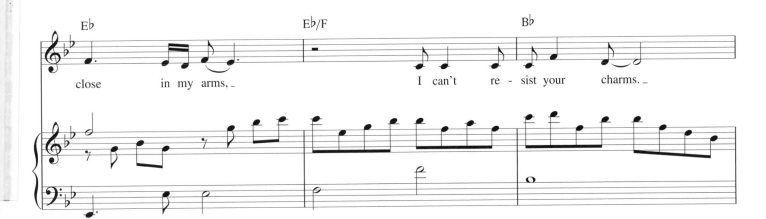

close in my arms, _ I can't re - sist your charms. _

And love, I'll be a

you · · · my end - less love.

And — love. —

I'll be that fool for you I'm

sure; you know I don't mind.

And yes, you'll be the

on - ly one. No one can de - ny

this love _____ I have in - side.   I'll

give _____ it all to you   my love, _ my love, _

___ my end - less love.

Grow Old with Me
Recorded by John Lennon

Words and Music by
John Lennon

Tenderly

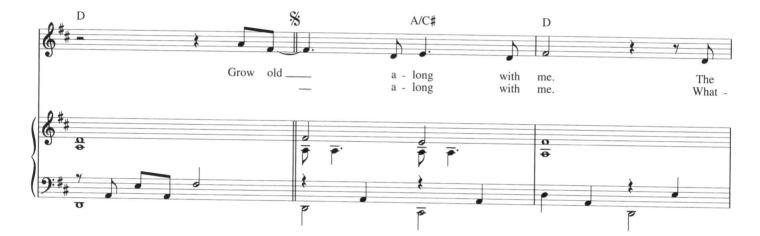

Grow old ____ a - long with me.
____ a - long with me. The
What -

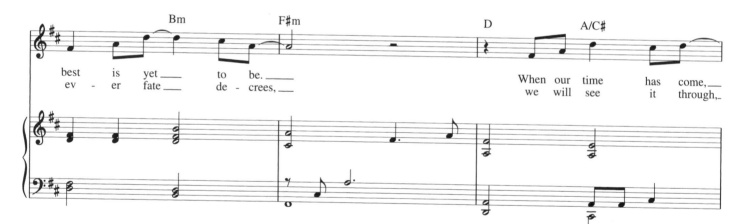

best is yet ____ to be. ____
ev - er fate ____ de - crees, ____
When our time has come, ____
we will see it through, ____

we will be as one. ____
for our love is true. ____

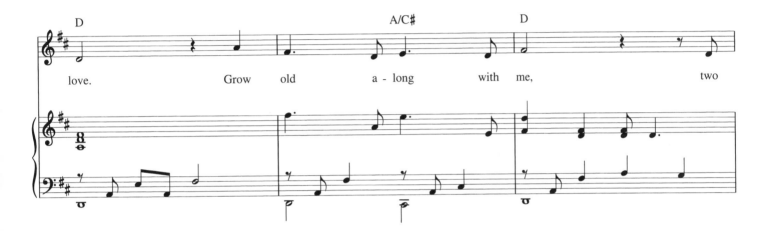

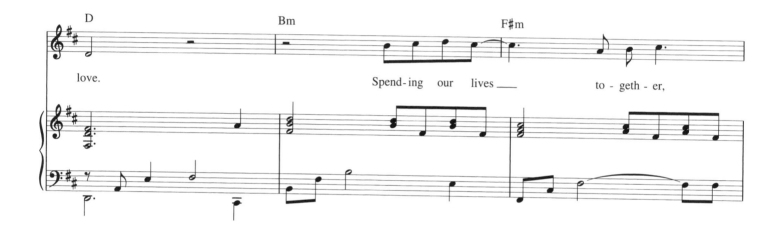

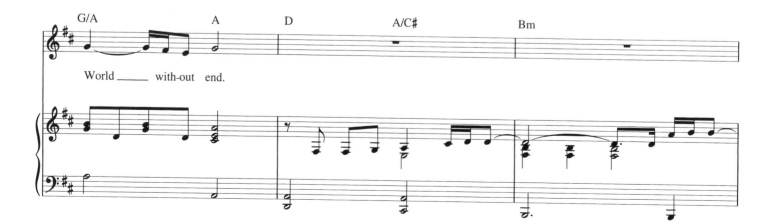

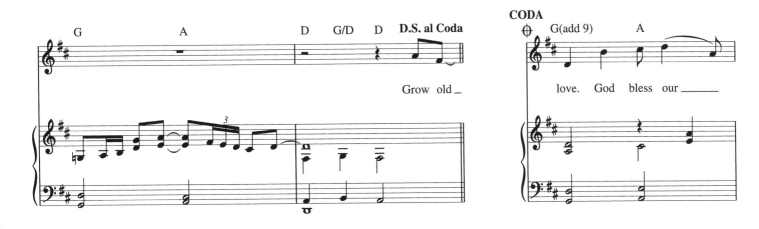

Grow old __

love. God bless our _____

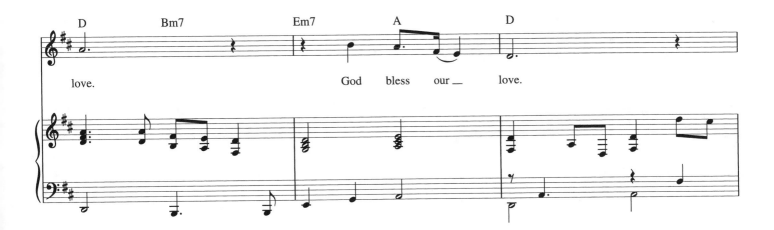

love.

God bless our __ love.

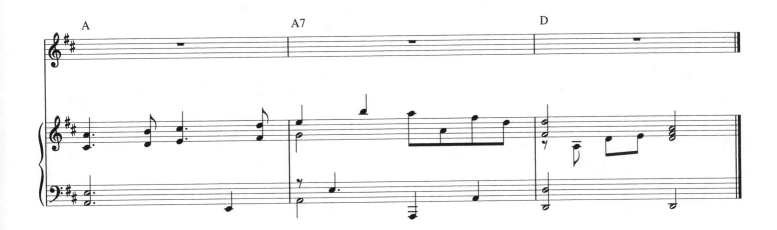

I Will

Recorded by The Beatles

Words and Music by John Lennon
and Paul McCartney

er real - ly mat - tered; I will al - ways feel ___ the same. ___

Love you for - ev - er and ___ for - ev - er, love you with all ___ my heart. ___

___ Love you when - ev - er we're ___ to - geth - er,

love you when we're ___ a - part. ___ And when ___ at last ___ I find ___

In My Life

Recorded by The Beatles

Words and Music by John Lennon
and Paul McCartney
Arranged by John Reed

still can re-call. __ Some are dead. and __ some __ are __ liv-ing; in my ___ life I've

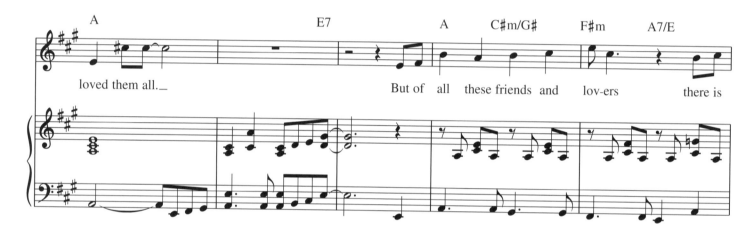

loved them all. __ But of all these friends and lov-ers there is

no __ one com-pares with you, __ and those mem-'ries lose their mean-ing when I think of __ love as

some-thing new. __ Tho' I know __ I'll __ nev-er lose af - fec-tion for peo-ple and things __ that

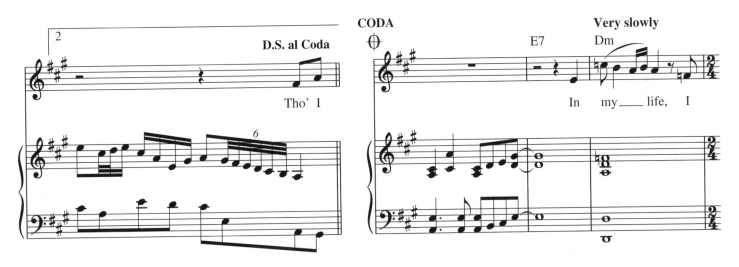

You Are So Beautiful

Recorded by Joe Cocker

Words and Music by Billy Preston
and Bruce Fisher

Moderately slow, expressively

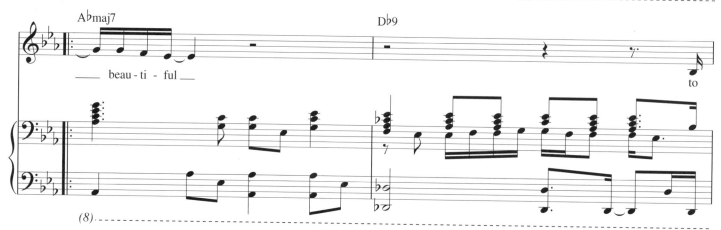

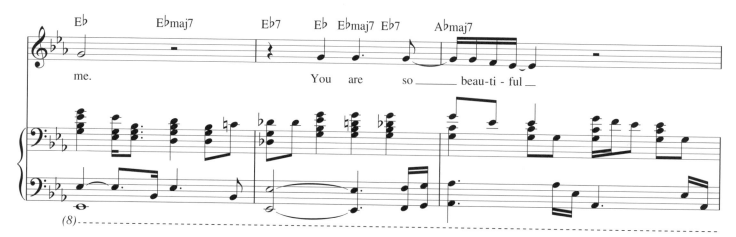

187

We've Only Just Begun

Recorded by The Carpenters

Words and Music by Roger Nichols
and Paul Williams

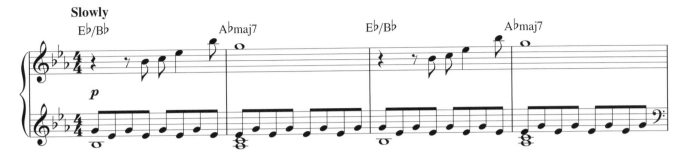

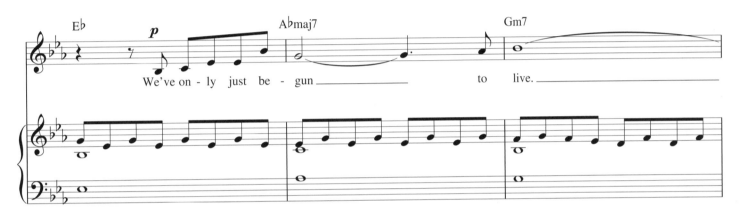

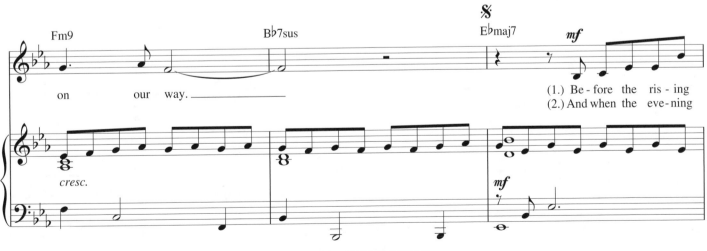

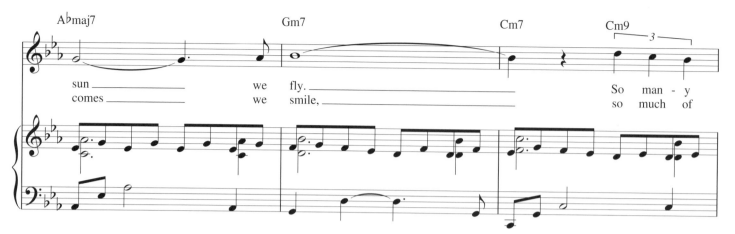

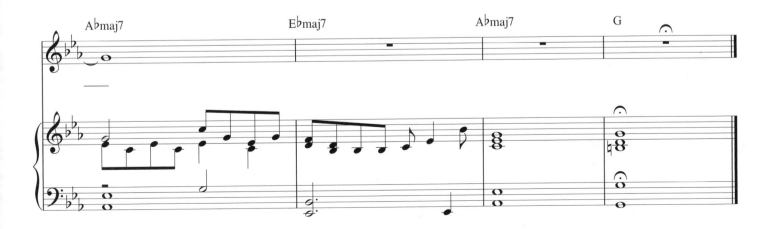

You Raise Me Up

Recorded by Josh Groban

Words and Music by Brendan Graham
and Rolf Lovland

When I am down ___ and oh, my soul's so

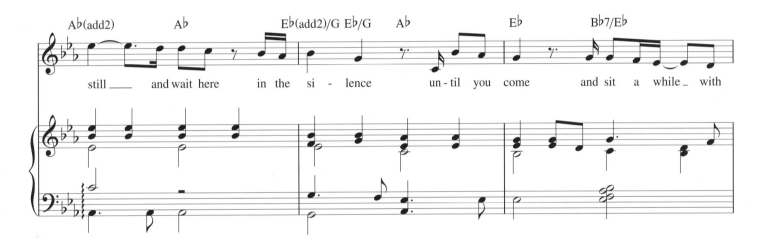

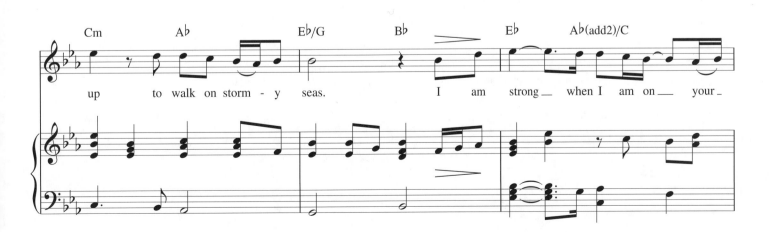

shoul - ders. You raise me up to more than I __ can be.

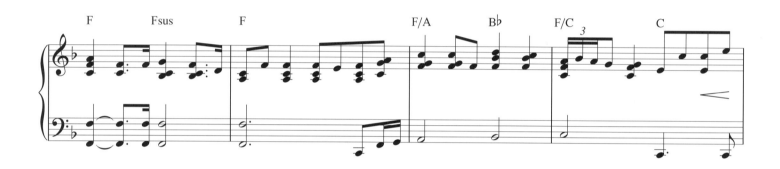

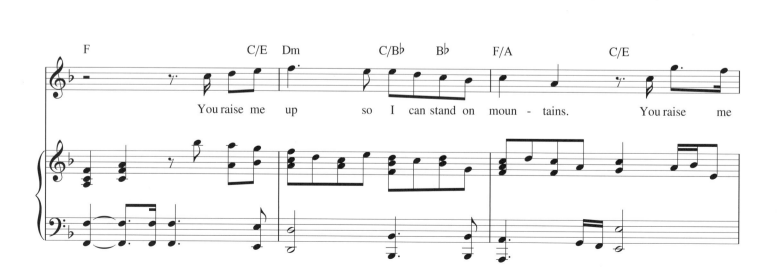

You raise me up so I can stand on moun - tains. You raise me

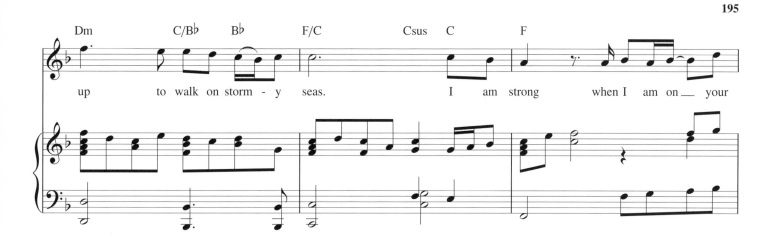

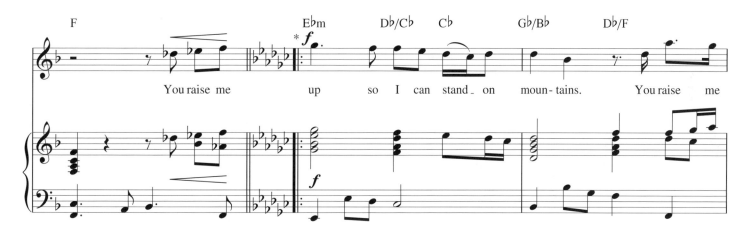

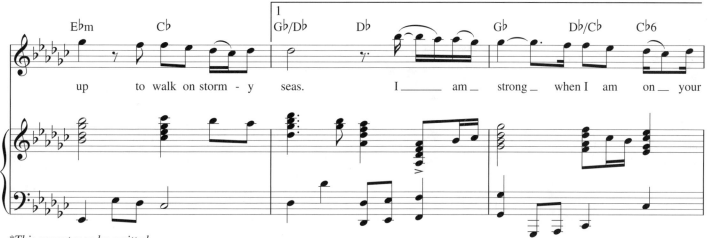

This repeat may be omitted.

If You Could See What I See

Recorded by Steven Curtis Chapman

Words and Music by Geoff Moore
and Steven Curtis Chapman

Romantically

With pedal

All of my life __
I know there are days __

__ I have dreamed __
__ when you feel _____

that some - how love __ would find me. __
so _____ much less __ than i - deal, __

Now I can't be-lieve ____ you're stand-ing here. __
won-der-ing what ____ I see in you.

If beau-ty is all ____
It's all of the light __

in the eye ____ of ____ the be-hold - er, then I __
and the grace; ____ your be-lief ____ in me drives __ me to say __

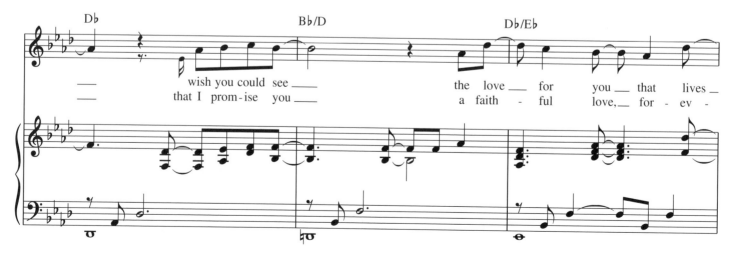

wish you could see ____ the love ____ for you __ that lives ____
that I prom-ise you ____ a faith - ful love, __ for - ev -

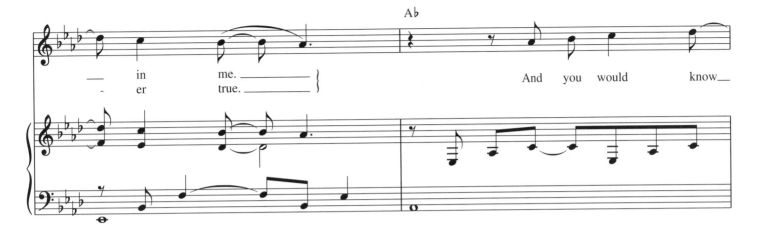

the on - ly one __ for me,

if you could see ____ what I see. ____

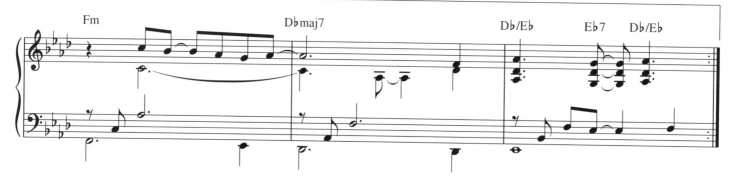

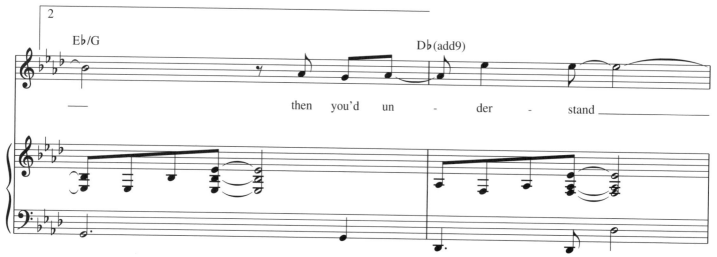

____ then you'd un - der - stand _____

How Beautiful

Recorded by Twila Paris

Words and Music by
Twila Paris

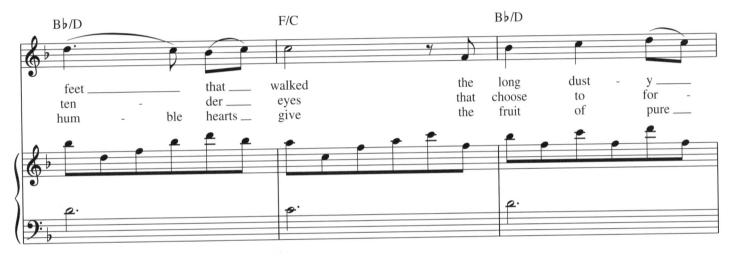

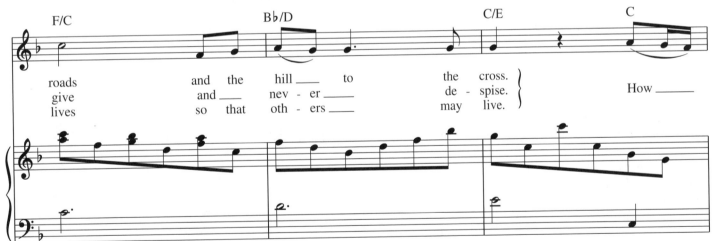

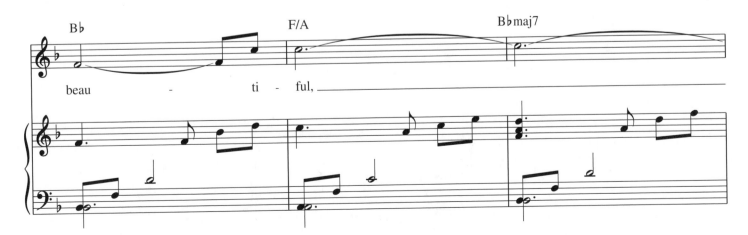

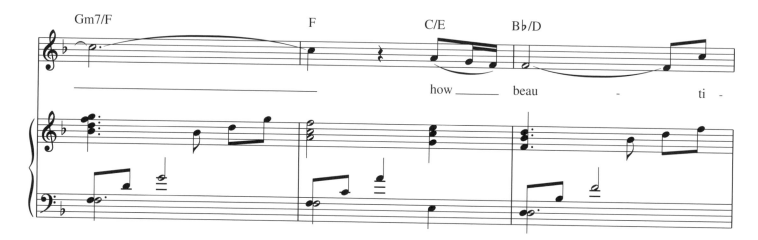

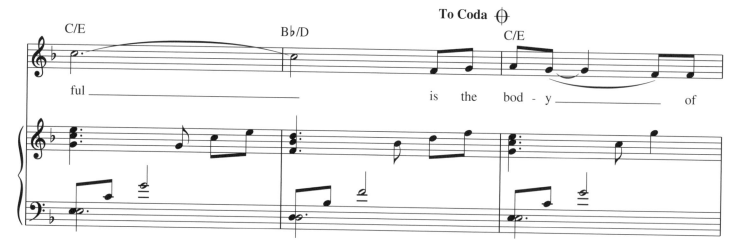

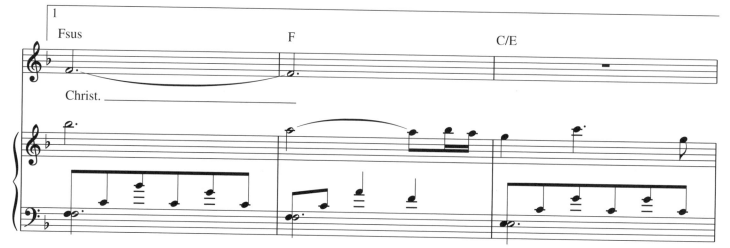

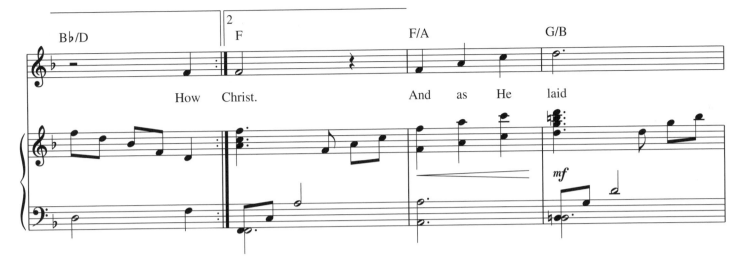

How Christ. And as He laid

down His life, we of - fer ___ this

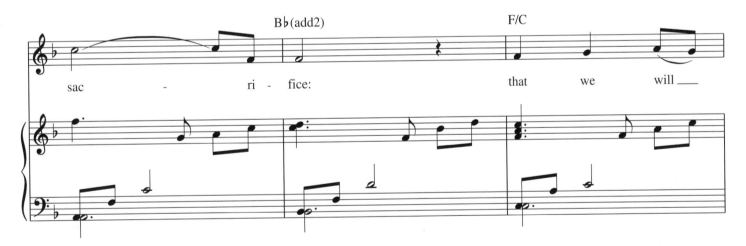

sac - ri - fice: that we will ___

live just as He ___ died,

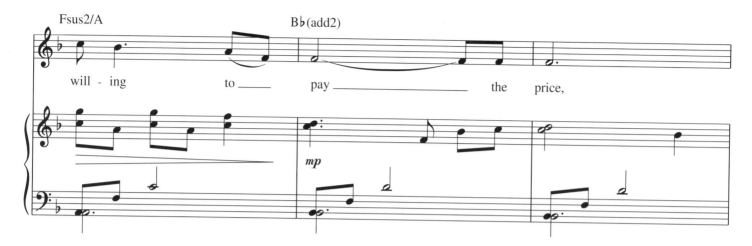

will - ing   to ____ pay _____ the   price,

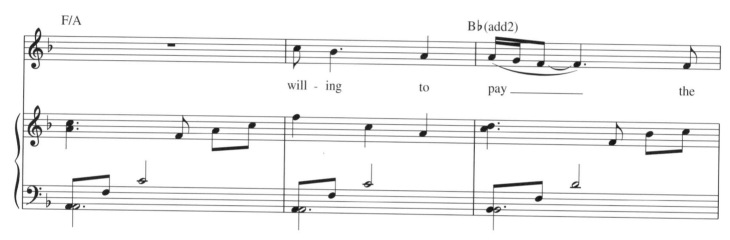

will - ing   to   pay _____   the

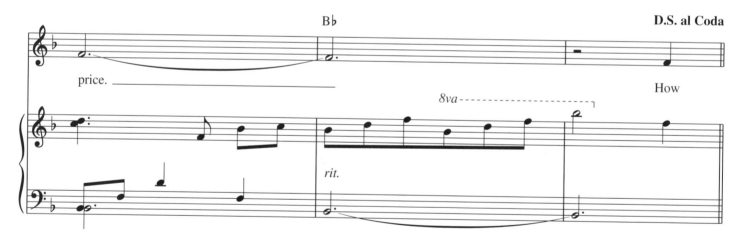

price. _____   How

D.S. al Coda

CODA

bod - y   of   Christ. _____

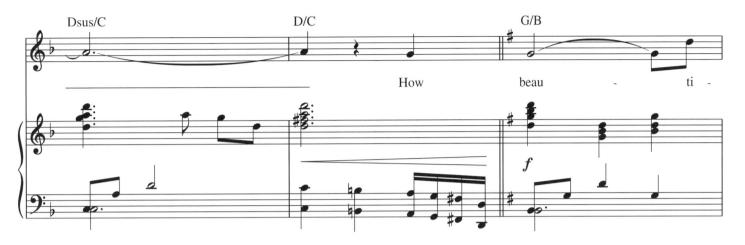

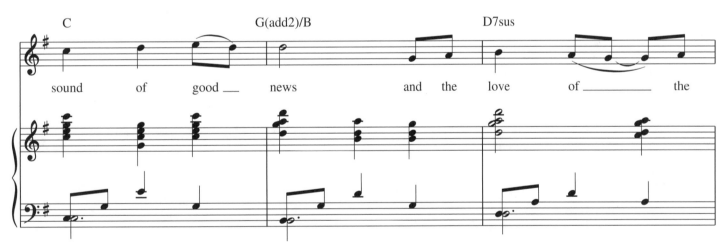

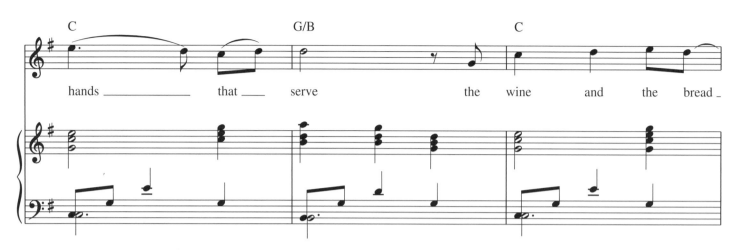

hands _____ that ___ serve the wine and the bread _

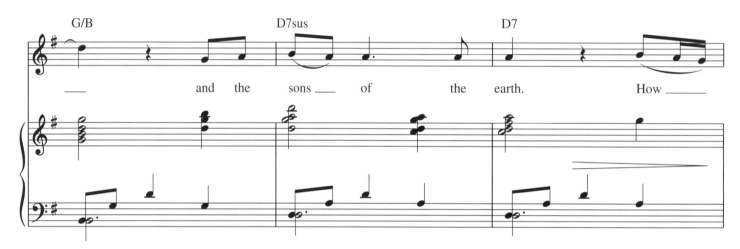

___ and the sons ___ of the earth. How _____

beau - ti - ful, _____

___ how _____ beau - ti - ful, _____

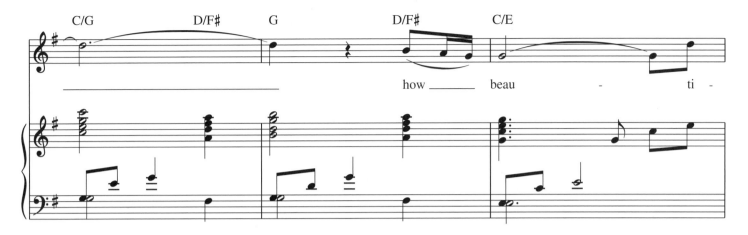

how _____ beau _____ ti -

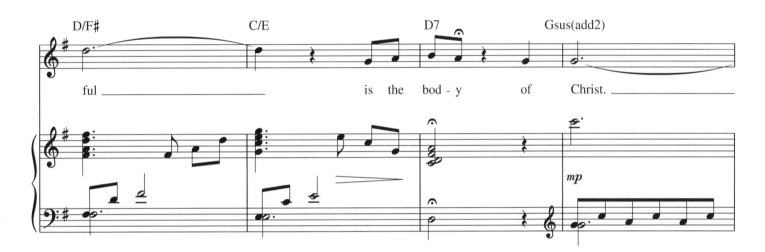

ful _____ is the bod - y of Christ. _____

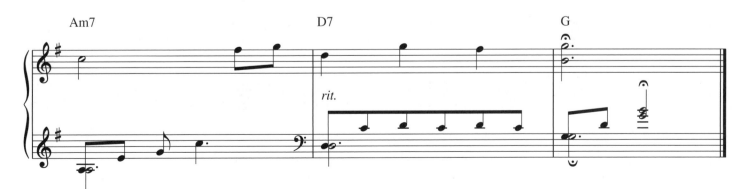

I Will Be Here

Recorded by Steven Curtis Chapman

Words and Music by
Steven Curtis Chapman

Moderately

Gently, but not too slowly

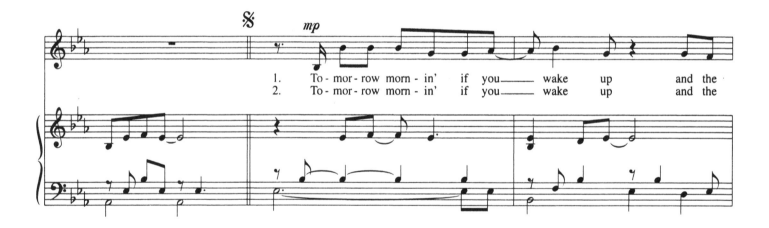

1. To - mor - row morn - in' if you____ wake up and the
2. To - mor - row morn - in' if you____ wake up and the

sun does____ not____ ap - pear,____ I,____
fu - ture is____ un - clear,____ I,____

I will be here.———
I will be here.———

If in the dark— we lose sight——— of— love,——— hold my—
As sure as sea-sons are made——— for— change,——— our

——hand and— have— no fear, 'cause I,———
life-times are made——— for— years, so I,———

I will be here.———
I will be here.———

I will be here—
I will be here—

when you feel like be - in' qui - et, when you
and you can cry on_____ my shoul - der when the

need to speak_____ your_____ mind,_____ I_____ will lis - ten, and I will be here.
mir - ror tells_____ us we're old - er I_____ will hold_____ you. And I will be here_____

When the laugh - ter turns_____ to cry - in', through the
to watch you grow_____ in beau - ty and tell you

2nd time to CODA ⊕

decresc.

win - nin', los - in' and try - in', we'll be to - geth - er,_____
all the things_____ you are to_____ me. I will be here._____

decresc.

D.S. al CODA

'cause I will be here.___

CODA

I will___ be___ true   to   the   prom -

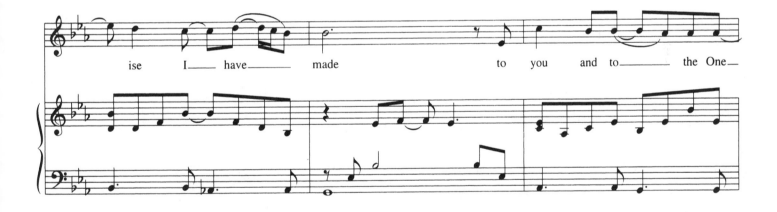

ise I___ have___ made   to   you   and to___   the One___

___   who gave you   to___   me.

I,_____ I will be here.___

And_____ just as sure as sea-sons are made___

___ for___ change,___ our life-times are made___ for___ years,_____ so

I,_____ I_____ will be_____

_____ here._____ We'll be to-geth-er._____

I will be____ here._____

Love of My Life

Recorded by Michael W. Smith

Words and Music by Jim Brickman
and Tom Douglas

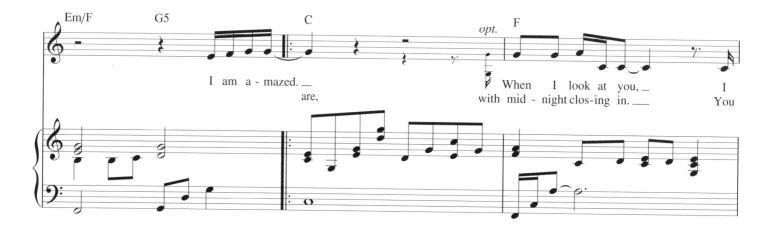

I am a-mazed. ___ are, When I look at you, ___ I
with mid-night clos-ing in. ___ You

see you smil-ing back at me. It's like all my dreams ___ come true. ___ I am a-fraid
take my hand as our shad-ows dance, with moon-light on ___ your skin. ___ I look in your eyes. ___

___ if I lost you girl, ___ I'd
___ I'm lost in-side your kiss. ___ I

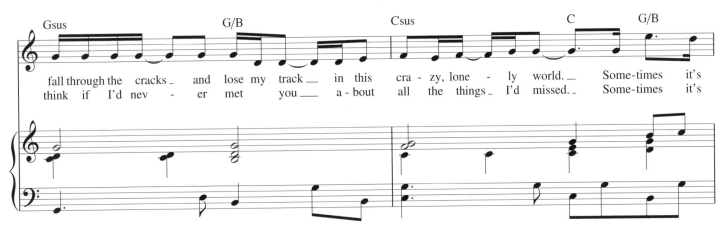

fall through the cracks___ and lose my track___ in this cra - zy, lone - ly world.___ Some-times it's
think if I'd nev - er met you___ a - bout all the things___ I'd missed.___ Some-times it's

so hard to be - lieve,___ when my nights can be___ so___ long,___ and
so hard to be - lieve,___ when a love can be___ so___ strong,__ and

faith gave me the strength_____ and kept me hold - ing on.___} You are the love_
faith gave me the strength_____ and kept me hold - ing on.___

___ of my life,___ and I'm so glad___ you found___ me. You are the love_

of my life. ___ Ba - by, put your arms ___ a - round ___ me. I ___ guess

this is how it feels ___ when you fin - 'lly find ___ some - thing real. ___ My

To Coda ⊕

an - gel in the night, ___ you are ___ my love, ___ the love of my

life.

Now, here you life.

You are the love ___
___ my an-gel in the night, ___ you are ___ my

love, the love of my life.

Parent's Prayer
(Let Go of Two)
Recorded by Steven Curtis Chapman

Words and Music by
Greg Davis

us _____ we have glad - ly passed _____ on to them. _____
ed _____ since the day You gave our chil - dren to us. _____

But one thing we don't _____ know is how to place them back in Your arms a - gain. _____
But now in Your arms, _____ dear Je - sus, the time has come for giv - ing them up. _____

Lord, help us let go of two _____ that they might _____ be - come one,

just like the Fa - ther, Spir - it and Son. _____ Two hearts in - vis - i - bly bound _____

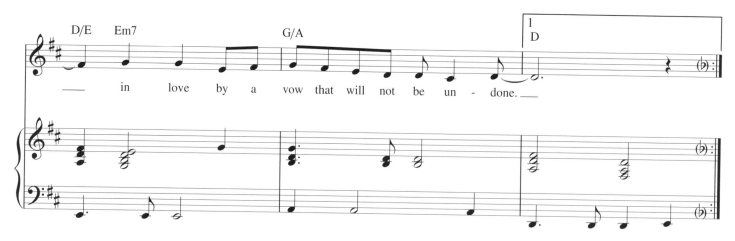

in love by a vow that will not be un - done. ___

___ The urge is strong ___ to try ___ hold-in' on ___ to the

im - age of two, ___ the way ___ that we knew them. But now in Your eyes the two ___

___ will be as ___ one. _____ Help us let go of two ___ that they might ___
(might ___

225

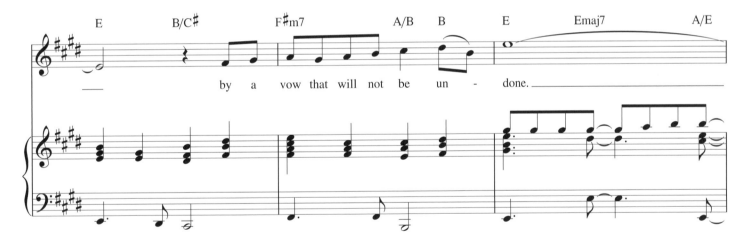

This Day
Recorded by Jadon Lavik

Words and Music by
Jadon Lavik

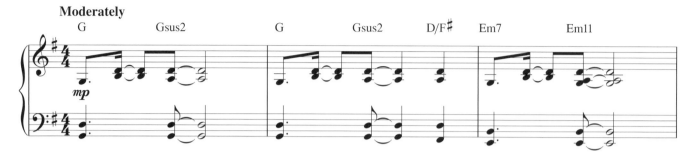

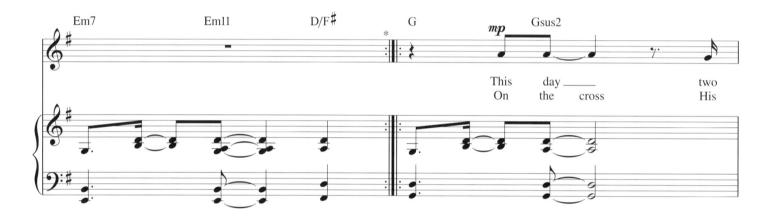

*This repeat may be omitted for a wedding.

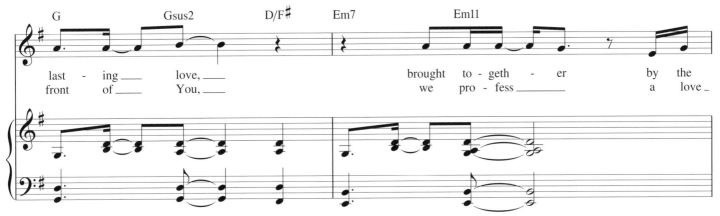

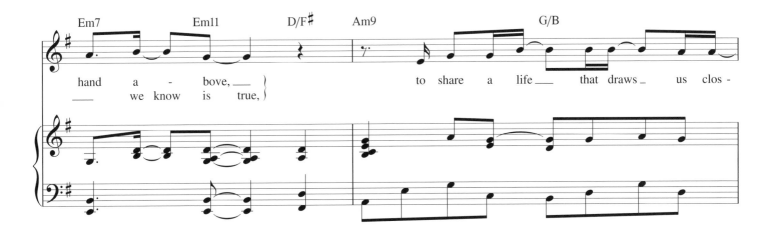

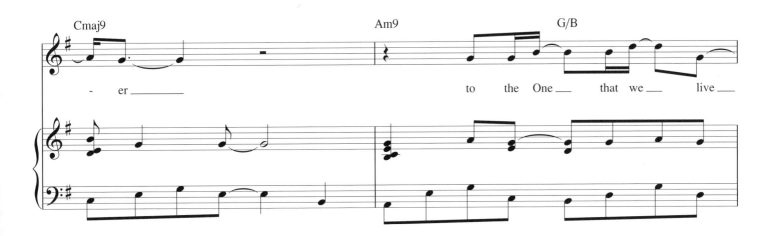

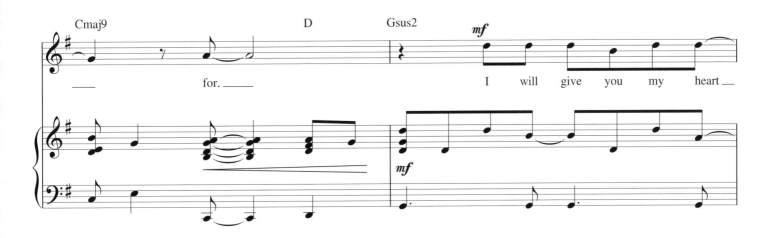

and all of who __ I am. __ I will give more than vows __

and words could ev - er say. __ Yes, I give __ you __ my all __

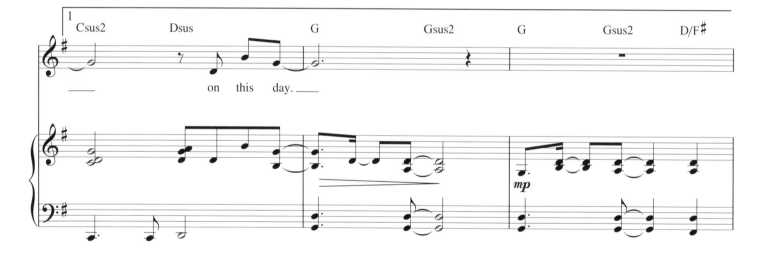

__ on this day. __

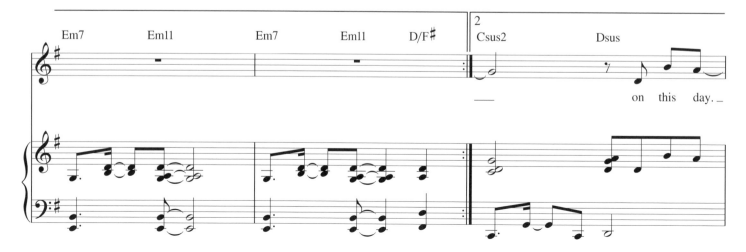

__ on this day. __

And I give _ you _ my all _ on this _ day. _

I will give you my heart _ and all of who _ I am. _

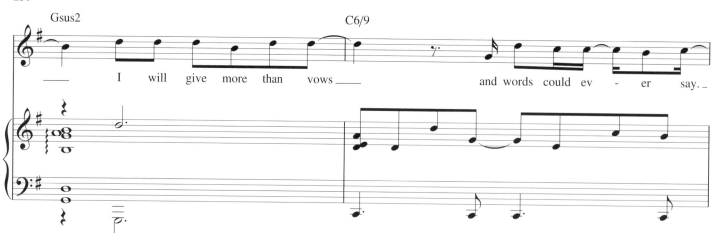

on this day. _____ And I'll give _____ you _____ my all _____

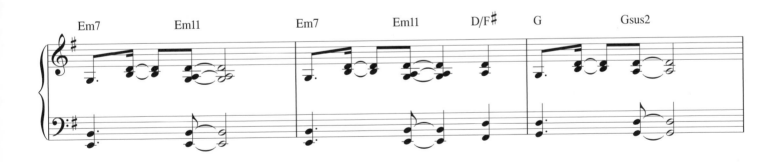

on this day. _____

This Is the Day
(A Wedding Song)
Recorded by Scott Wesley Brown

Words and Music by
Scott Wesley Brown

Moderately fast, flowing

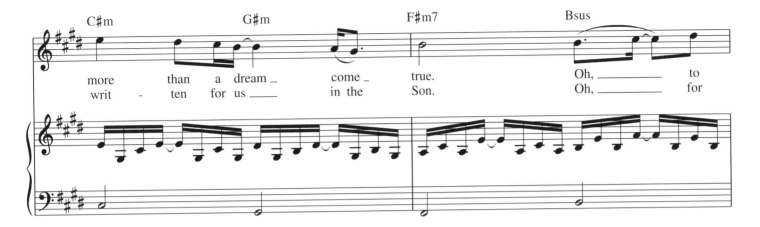

more than a dream ___ come ___ true.
writ - ten for us ___ in the Son.
Oh, _____ to
Oh, _____ for

have you, to hold ___ you, ___ to love you, to pray, ___ to
bet - ter, for worse, _____ for rich or for poor; ___

share with, to care ___ with, to hold hands ___ and say: _____
each day that pass - es I'll love ___ you more, _____ 'cause

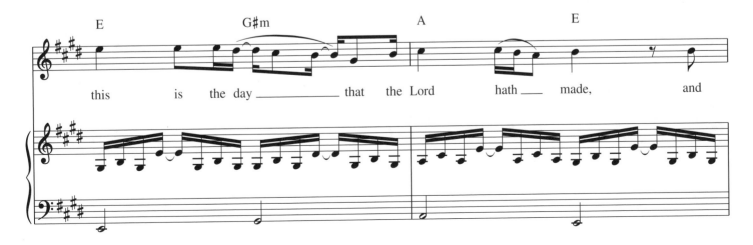

this is the day _____ that the Lord hath ___ made, and

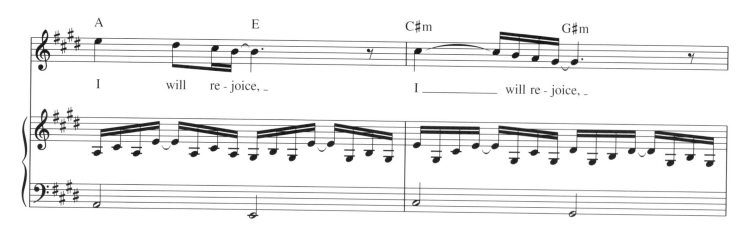

I will re - joice, _ I _____ will re - joice, _

I _____ will re - joice _ with you.

you. This is the day, _

this is the day, _

My Place Is With You

Recorded by Clay Crosse

Words and Music by Michael Puryear
and Geoffrey Thurman

I've walked a-long a hun-dred high-ways, ___
I've had my prom-is-es ___ for-sak-en ___

some I wish ___ I could for-get. ___
in too man-y emp-ty words. ___

And I've burned a lot ___ of bridg-es ___
And I'm a-mazed and so ___ a-stound-ed ___

but there's not one ___ that I ___ re-gret. ___
that I won't get ___ what I ___ de-serve. ___

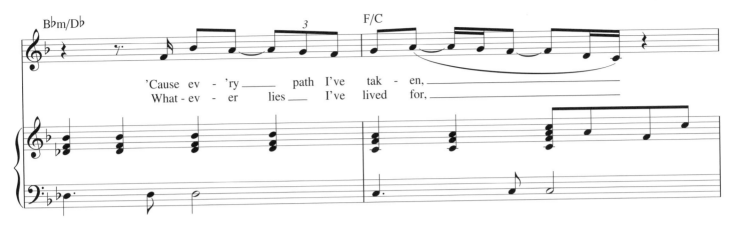

'Cause ev - 'ry _____ path I've tak - en, _____
What - ev - er lies _____ I've lived for, _____

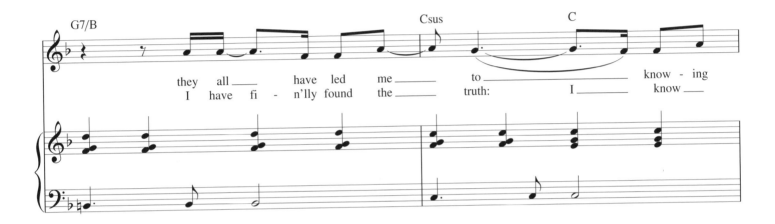

they all _____ have led me _____ to _____ know - ing
I have fi - n'lly found the _____ truth: I _____ know _____

my _____ place, _ my place _ is with you. _____
my _____ place, _ my place _ is with you.

You are my

treas - ure ___ for - ev - er, the ___ one dream I've ___ searched for. ___

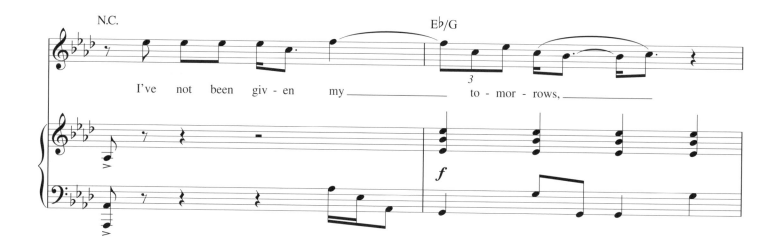

I've not been giv - en my ___ to - mor - rows, ___

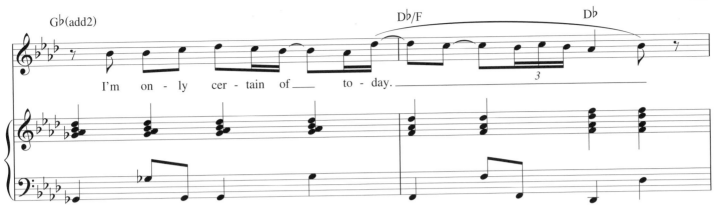

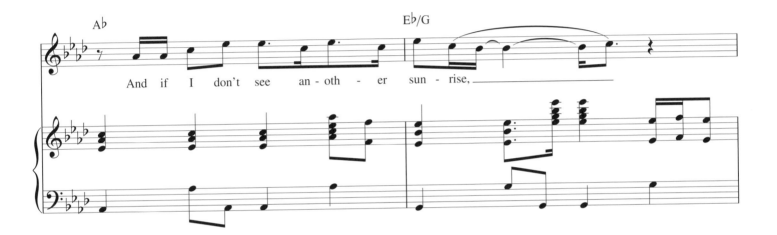

when all ___ my days _____ are through. _____ I _____ know _

my _____ place, _____ my place _ is with you. ___

My place _ is with you. _____ My place _ is with you. _

My place ___ is with you.